SEW JEWISH

SEW JEWISH

The 18 Projects You Need for Jewish Holidays,
Weddings, Bar/Bat Mitzvah Celebrations and Home

M. Bywater

Sew Jewish ™

Sew Jewish: The 18 Projects You Need for Jewish Holidays, Weddings, Bar/Bat Mitzvah Celebrations and Home
©Copyright 2016 by Maria Bywater

Sew Jewish LLC
New York
SewJewish.com

Educators: Sew Jewish encourages you to use this book for educational purposes, consistent with the restrictions stated above. Contact Sew Jewish for information about discounts for educators and their students at info@sewjewish.com.

The information in this book is provided in good faith, but no warranty is given and no results are guaranteed. Because Sew Jewish does not have control over the materials and techniques used, the company assumes no responsibility for the use of this information.

ISBN: 978-0-9968582-0-5 [PDF]
ISBN: 978-0-9968582-2-9 [Softcover]
Library of Congress Control Number: 2015915827

Credits:
Project Photos: Matzah cover, wedding huppah, kippah, tallit, tallit bag, shalom pillow by Kat DeLeon; Others by Maria Bywater
Author Photo: Erin Frances

Contents

If you're a beginning sewing enthusiast, start by taking a look at all the helpful info here!

Introduction

May the favor of the Lord, our God, be upon us; let the work of our hands prosper. (Psalms 90:17)

The first official Jewish sewing project in history was the Tabernacle, or Tent of Meeting, which the Israelites built after emerging from slavery in Egypt. The tent housed the Ark of the Covenant with the tablets on which the Ten Commandments were written. It was a place for the priests to perform their duties and a place for Moses to meet with God.

Following instructions detailed in the Torah and explained by God to Moses, the Israelites sewed coverings of animal skins to drape over the top of the tent's wooden walls. They spun wool to weave curtains, and they embroidered the curtains with images of angels.

"Let them make Me a sanctuary," God told Moses, "that I may dwell among them" (Exodus 25:8). Most commentaries on this Torah passage assume that it was the tent itself that enabled God to dwell among the Israelites. But one of my favorite commentaries takes a closer look at the words God uses here. It's not the tent itself that enables God to dwell among the Israelites, the commentary concludes, but the Israelites' act of making it.

As someone who's spent countless hours sewing, that idea resonates with me, as I'm sure it does for anyone who has created something by hand. By bringing something into existence with our own hands, we become invested in it. A God who could part the Red Sea surely could have given the Israelites a completed Tabernacle—or given us a completed tallit or challah cover for that matter. But by making something ourselves the product takes on more meaning than it would if someone gave it to us or we bought it ready made.

In the three or four thousand years since the Israelites built the Tabernacle, Jewish life has expanded and grown richer, and so have Jewish needlecrafts. For this book, I've selected 18 projects that touch the heart of Jewish life. You'll find projects to take you through the calendar of Jewish holidays, to celebrate weddings and bar and bat mitzvahs, and to bring warmth to your home. Some of the projects connect directly to Biblical commandments, such as the tallit and the mezuzah case. You'll find ritual objects for your home, such as the Passover matzah cover and hand washing towel. You'll find projects that link to Jewish tradition and identity, such as the kippah and wedding huppah, and to folk practices, like the hamsa. And you'll find items that express traditional Jewish communal values, like the tzedakah jar for collecting money for charity and a cuddly kids' blanket to introduce the letters of the Hebrew aleph-bet to the next generation. Some of these projects are the first of their kind that we've seen rendered in fabric, like the mezuzah case and the tzedakah jar wrap. Two of them, the mezuzah case and tefillin bag, have the potential, according to Jewish teaching, to become holy objects.

My path in designing and sewing Judaica includes designing wedding huppahs for Huppahs.com, making tallits, and blogging at Sew Jewish (sewjewish.com). This *Sew Jewish* book enables me to show you how to make key pieces of Judaica for your life and home.

If you know how to set your sewing machine to a straight stitch and a zigzag stitch, you can make all the projects in the book. The instructions include lots of support, especially with beginner sewists in mind. In the last section of the book, Basic Techniques, you'll find help with introductory topics such as choosing fabrics and cutting fabric as well as techniques such as making appliques and embroidering. You'll even find video tutorials on the Sew Jewish channel on YouTube and helpful posts on the Sew Jewish blog (SewJewish.com).

 Throughout the book, the Sew Jewish angel will give you plenty of tips—the kind of tips I'd give you if I was in the same room with you teaching you how to sew these projects.

You don't need to be Jewish to make these projects. It's my hope that everyone who finds this book will be inspired to make something for themselves or someone in their life.

All of these projects are here for you. Make them your own. The tradition is in your hands.

Dedication

To my daughters, Clara and Agnes. You inspire me every day.

Key to Illustrations

Fabric and Materials

| Right Side of Fabric | Wrong Side of Fabric | Interfacing/ Craft Backing |

Gray = The right side of the fabric, the side that will show on the outside of the finished project. For projects consisting of only one layer of fabric, such as the tallit, it's the side that faces up or faces out when the finished project is used.

White = The wrong side of the fabric, the side that doesn't show in the finished project. For projects with only one layer of fabric, it's the side that faces down or in when the project is used.

Interfacing/Craft Backing = These textiles add body to a project. Most of the illustrations won't show these materials, but when they do, they'll look like this.

Pattern Markings

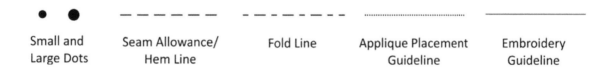

Small and Large Dots   Seam Allowance/ Hem Line   Fold Line   Applique Placement Guideline   Embroidery Guideline

Shabbat and Holidays

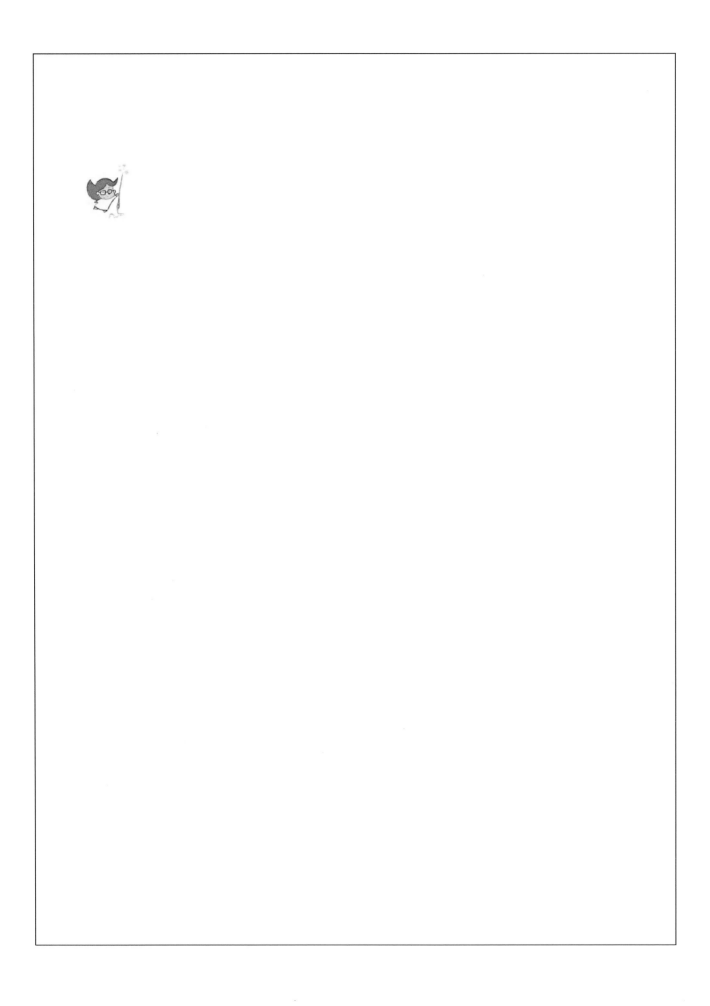

Challah Cover

...In the morning there was a fall of dew about the [Israelites'] camp. When the fall of dew lifted, there over the surface of the wilderness lay a fine and flaky substance, as fine as frost on the ground. When the Israelites saw it, they said to one another, "What is it?"—for they did not know what it was. And Moses said to them, "That is the bread which the Lord has given you to eat..." (Exodus 16:13-15)

If the table is the center of Jewish family holidays, then the challah cover is the centerpiece. When we sit down to Shabbat and festival meals, the cover lies over two loaves of challah bread, recalling the dew that covered the bread that God provided for the Israelites in the desert. This challah cover features the traditional Hebrew phrase *"Shabbat v'yom tov,"* which means "Shabbat and holiday," making it suitable for Shabbat and all of the holidays except Passover. On classic Old World challah covers the phrase is often embroidered in gold. Here, the letters are appliqued, a technique that's faster and easier than hand embroidery and adds a solid shot of color to a modern table.

Final size: 22" x 18" (55.9cm x 45.7cm)

Materials

Recommended fabrics: Medium weight satin, Dupioni silk, shantung

Fabric:

Cover: 3/8 yd. (40cm) at least 35" (90cm) wide

Border and appliques: 5/8 yd. (60cm) at least 45" (115cm) wide **OR** ½ yd. (50cm) at least 54" (137cm) wide

Light or medium weight non-stretch fusible tricot interfacing

Special Equipment

Transfer paper

Water or air erasable fabric marker

Sharp machine needle, such as Shmetz microtex sharp needles

 Tip: The instructions call for silk and silk-like fabrics, but you could also use cotton or linen. If you do, use iron-on adhesive web instead of tricot interfacing for the appliques, and follow the instructions in Basic Techniques: Making Appliques from Cotton and Linen Fabrics on page 140.

Instructions

Copy the Pattern

Copy or trace the pattern pages for the cover, long border, and short border—you'll find them at the end of the instructions (for tips, see Basic Techniques: Copying and Tracing Patterns on page 137).

Cut out the pattern pieces and tape them together using the guidelines.

Cut the Fabric

Cover Fabric: Cut two copies of the cover pattern. Use the transfer paper to transfer the dots to the right side of the cover pieces (see Basic Techniques: Transferring Pattern Markings on page 139).

Border/Applique Fabric: Cut two copies each of the long border and short border patterns, reserving some fabric for the appliques. Use the diagrams on the next page for help fitting all the pieces on the fabric, depending on the fabric width.

45" (115cm) Wide

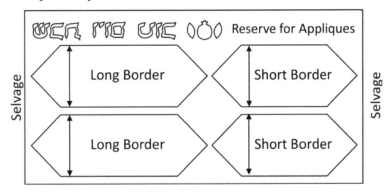

54" (137cm) Wide

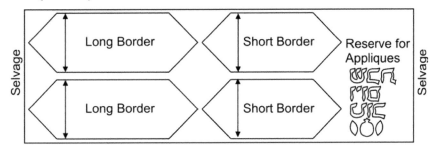

Transfer the dots on the pattern to the wrong sides of the border pieces.

Make the Appliques

On one of the cover pieces, use the erasable fabric marker to trace the applique guidelines from the pattern onto the right side of the fabric. Use close zigzag stitches to finish the edges of this cover piece.

Create appliques for the letters, pomegranate, and leaves using the reserved border fabric, the tricot interfacing, and the applique patterns (see Basic Techniques: Machine Applique, Making Appliques from Silk and Silk-like Fabrics on page 141).

 Pomegranates are native to the Land of Israel and have a deep, rich history in Jewish design.

Baste the appliques in place on the cover.

 Tip: Cut out and finish one line of appliques at a time. You'll minimize the chance of misplacing any of the appliques before attaching them to the cover while also preventing unfinished appliques from fraying at the edges while you work on other sections of the design.

Finish the Appliques

Insert the sharp needle into your machine. Finish the edges of the appliques with close, medium width zigzag stitches (see Basic Techniques: Machine Applique, Finishing Machine Appliques on page 142).

 Tip: The sharp needle will minimize holes in your silk fabric.

Sew the Cover Pieces Together

Note: Use a ½" (1.2cm) seam allowance throughout.

With wrong sides together and matching the dots, sew the cover pieces together ½" (1.2cm) from the edges.

Make the Border

With right sides together, sew one long and one short border piece together along one pointed end between the dots.

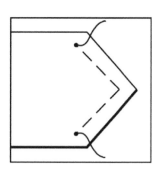

Clip the corners and grade the seam allowance.

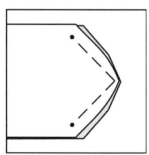

Use the same technique to sew all four border pieces together end to end to make a frame, alternating long and short pieces.

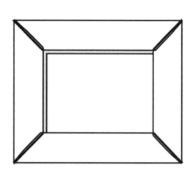

Press the seams open. If you find it difficult to press the seams open all the way to the corner, try to press to at least ½" (1.2cm) from the corner.

 Tip: If you are using Dupioni silk, shantung, or other textured fabric, press lightly or place a cloth between the fabric and iron to avoid flattening the texture.

Attach the Border to the Cover

With right sides together, pin one long edge of a long border piece to one long edge of the non-appliqued side of the cover, matching edges and dots. Make sure the seam allowances lie flat. Sew between the dots.

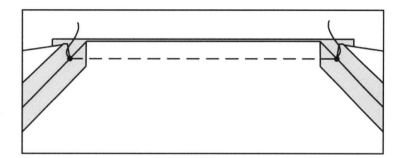

Sew the two short border pieces and the remaining long border piece to the cover in the same way, one side at a time, each time matching edges and dots.

Press the seam allowances toward the border.

Press under the free edges of the border pieces ½" (1.2 cm) from the edge.

Turn the pressed edges of the border to the front of the cover so that they just cover the stitches. Pin the border in place. Sew the border to the cover around all four sides 1/8" (3mm) from the pressed edge.

Press.

Pattern

Cover
Challah Cover

Cut 2 from Fabric

The completed cover pattern looks like this:

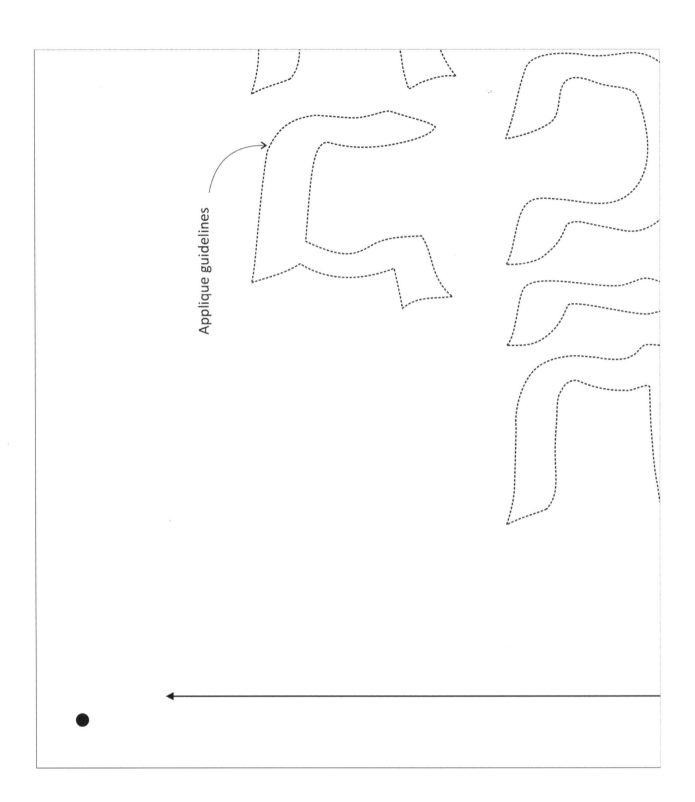

Applique guidelines

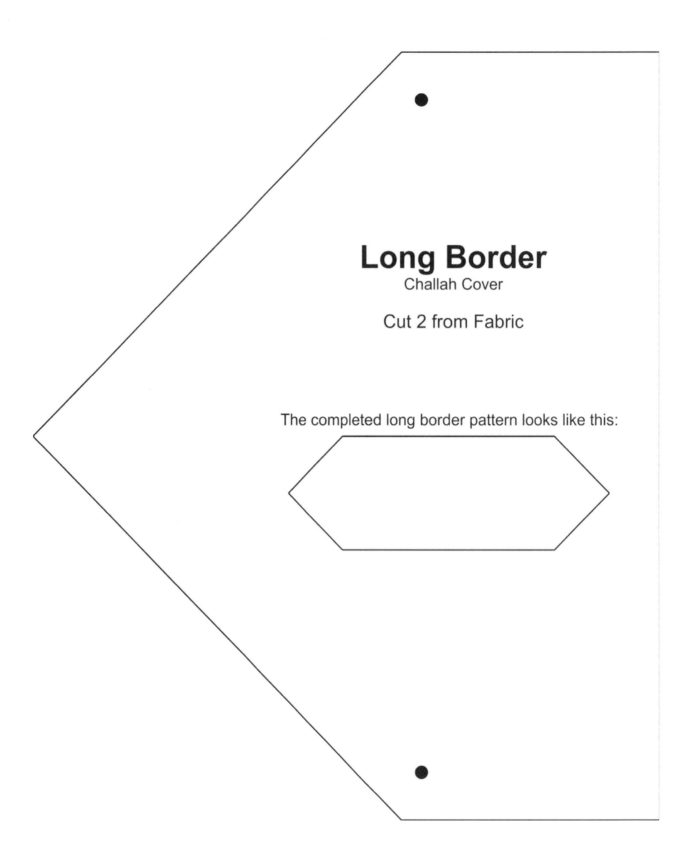

Long Border
Challah Cover

Cut 2 from Fabric

The completed long border pattern looks like this:

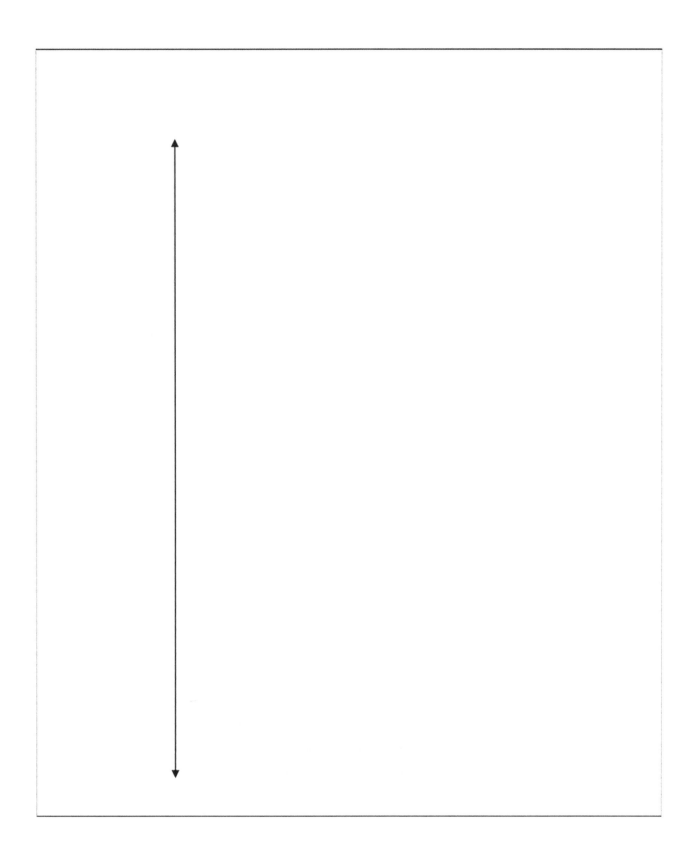

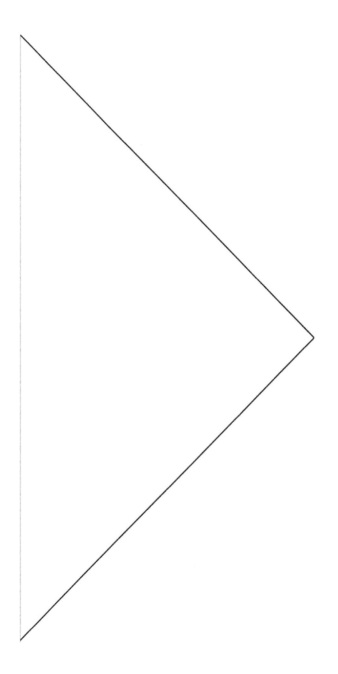

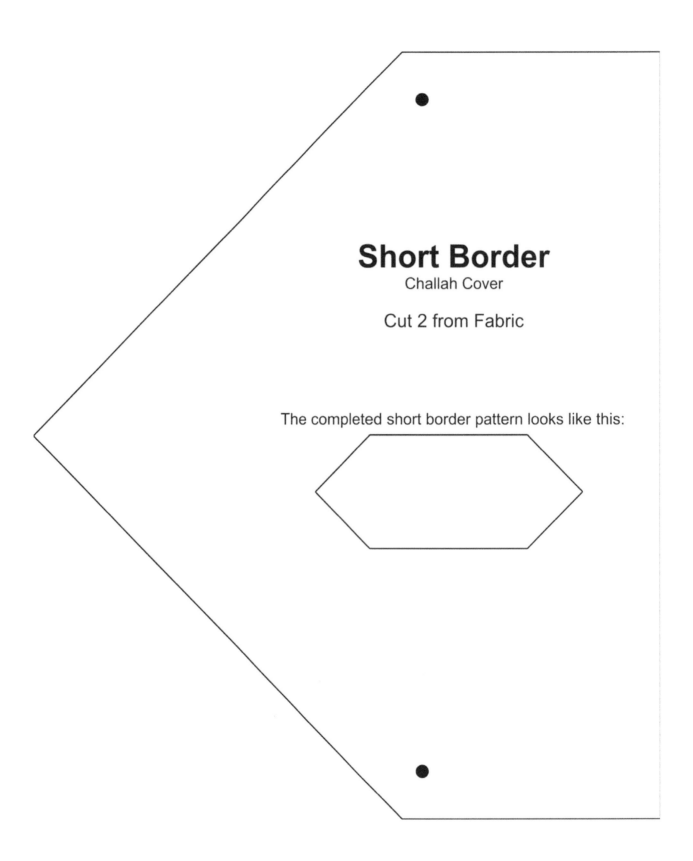

Short Border
Challah Cover

Cut 2 from Fabric

The completed short border pattern looks like this:

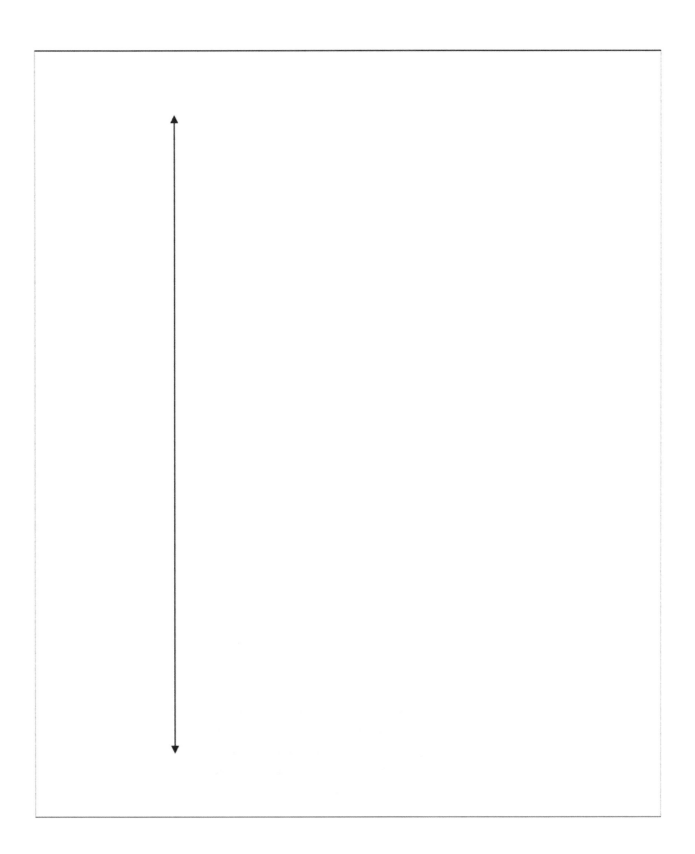

Applique Patterns

Hanukkah Dreidel Game Kits

A great miracle happened there.—Dreidel game

Hanukkah celebrates the miracle that happened two thousand years ago after a group of Jewish soldiers called Maccabees liberated the Temple in Jerusalem from foreign forces. A jar of oil for lighting the Temple menorah, which should have lasted for only one day, lasted for eight days. I doubt the Maccabees guessed we'd celebrate Hanukkah by playing dreidel. Or that we'd make dreidel game kits like these. But I'm sure that if they saw them they'd want one. We're starting with purchased organza bags, which you'll find everywhere during the holiday season—craft stores, gift stores, even many grocery stores—and they'll save you lots of time. Then we refine the bags with a couple of well-placed seams so they stand up straight, like a troop of Maccabean soldiers. Hand the kits out as Hanukkah party favors, or tie name tags to the drawstrings to make place cards for a sit-down party. My favorite idea: For a holiday cocktail party, serve them on a tray as if they're one of the passed hors d'oeuvres.

Finished size: Determined by size of purchased bags

Materials

Organza bags with drawstrings, 3" x 4" (7.6cm x 10.1cm) or larger
Thread
Purchased dreidels, one for each bag
Purchased gelt (chocolate coins), candy, or other small treats, 6-8 per bag

Instructions

Sew the Bottoms of the Bags

Turn one bag inside out.

Depending on how your bags were made, the seams will lie along the sides of the bag or along the bottom. Flatten one bottom corner so that the side seam or fold lies directly on top of the bottom seam or fold.

Sew across the flattened corner in a straight line 5/8" (1.5cm) from the corner.

 Tip: To measure easily, place the flattened corner under your sewing machine's presser foot with the tip of the corner even with the 5/8" (1.5cm) line on the throat plate.

Sew across the other bottom corner in the same way.

Turn the bag right side out.

Sew the remaining bags in the same way.

Add the Fun Bits

Add the gelt or other treats and a dreidel to each bag.

Copy the game instructions for outside Israel or inside Israel, depending on where you live.

 Tip: There are lots of variations on the dreidel game. This is one of the simpler versions.

Cut the instruction cards along the lines, fold them, and insert them into the bags.

Pull the drawstrings to close.

Dreidel Game Instructions – Outside Israel

 Tip: Outside of Israel, the Hebrew letters on the dreidel—nun, gimmel, hay, and shin—are the first letters in the words of the Hebrew sentence "Nes gadol hayah sham," which means "A great miracle happened there." It refers to the Hanukkah miracle in which the menorah in the Temple burned for eight days with only one day's worth of oil.

The Dreidel Game

All players put one piece of gelt into the middle, "the pot". Players take turns spinning the dreidel:

נ Nun: Player wins nothing.

ג Gimmel: Player wins the whole pot. Everyone puts in another piece.

ה Hay: Player wins half the pot.

ש Shin: Player puts one piece of gelt in the pot.

When all your gelt is gone, you're out.

The Dreidel Game

All players put one piece of gelt into the middle, "the pot". Players take turns spinning the dreidel:

נ Nun: Player wins nothing.

ג Gimmel: Player wins the whole pot. Everyone puts in another piece.

ה Hay: Player wins half the pot.

ש Shin: Player puts one piece of gelt in the pot.

When all your gelt is gone, you're out.

The Dreidel Game

All players put one piece of gelt into the middle, "the pot". Players take turns spinning the dreidel:

נ Nun: Player wins nothing.

ג Gimmel: Player wins the whole pot. Everyone puts in another piece.

ה Hay: Player wins half the pot.

ש Shin: Player puts one piece of gelt in the pot.

When all your gelt is gone, you're out.

The Dreidel Game

All players put one piece of gelt into the middle, "the pot". Players take turns spinning the dreidel:

נ Nun: Player wins nothing.

ג Gimmel: Player wins the whole pot. Everyone puts in another piece.

ה Hay: Player wins half the pot.

ש Shin: Player puts one piece of gelt in the pot.

When all your gelt is gone, you're out.

The Dreidel Game

All players put one piece of gelt into the middle, "the pot". Players take turns spinning the dreidel:

נ Nun: Player wins nothing.

ג Gimmel: Player wins the whole pot. Everyone puts in another piece.

ה Hay: Player wins half the pot.

ש Shin: Player puts one piece of gelt in the pot.

When all your gelt is gone, you're out.

The Dreidel Game

All players put one piece of gelt into the middle, "the pot". Players take turns spinning the dreidel:

נ Nun: Player wins nothing.

ג Gimmel: Player wins the whole pot. Everyone puts in another piece.

ה Hay: Player wins half the pot.

ש Shin: Player puts one piece of gelt in the pot.

When all your gelt is gone, you're out.

The Dreidel Game

All players put one piece of gelt into the middle, "the pot". Players take turns spinning the dreidel:

נ Nun: Player wins nothing.

ג Gimmel: Player wins the whole pot. Everyone puts in another piece.

ה Hay: Player wins half the pot.

ש Shin: Player puts one piece of gelt in the pot.

When all your gelt is gone, you're out.

The Dreidel Game

All players put one piece of gelt into the middle, "the pot". Players take turns spinning the dreidel:

נ Nun: Player wins nothing.

ג Gimmel: Player wins the whole pot. Everyone puts in another piece.

ה Hay: Player wins half the pot.

ש Shin: Player puts one piece of gelt in the pot.

When all your gelt is gone, you're out.

The Dreidel Game

All players put one piece of gelt into the middle, "the pot". Players take turns spinning the dreidel:

נ Nun: Player wins nothing.

ג Gimmel: Player wins the whole pot. Everyone puts in another piece.

ה Hay: Player wins half the pot.

ש Shin: Player puts one piece of gelt in the pot.

When all your gelt is gone, you're out.

The Dreidel Game

All players put one piece of gelt into the middle, "the pot". Players take turns spinning the dreidel:

נ Nun: Player wins nothing.

ג Gimmel: Player wins the whole pot. Everyone puts in another piece.

ה Hay: Player wins half the pot.

ש Shin: Player puts one piece of gelt in the pot.

When all your gelt is gone, you're out.

The Dreidel Game

All players put one piece of gelt into the middle, "the pot". Players take turns spinning the dreidel:

נ Nun: Player wins nothing.

ג Gimmel: Player wins the whole pot. Everyone puts in another piece.

ה Hay: Player wins half the pot.

ש Shin: Player puts one piece of gelt in the pot.

When all your gelt is gone, you're out.

The Dreidel Game

All players put one piece of gelt into the middle, "the pot". Players take turns spinning the dreidel:

נ Nun: Player wins nothing.

ג Gimmel: Player wins the whole pot. Everyone puts in another piece.

ה Hay: Player wins half the pot.

ש Shin: Player puts one piece of gelt in the pot.

When all your gelt is gone, you're out.

Dreidel Game Instructions – Inside Israel

 Tip: Inside Israel, the dreidel shows the Hebrew letter pey instead of shin, to stand for the sentence "Nes gadol hayah poh," which means "A great miracle happened here."

The Dreidel Game

All players put one piece of gelt into the middle, "the pot". Players take turns spinning the dreidel:

נ Nun: Player wins nothing.

ג Gimmel: Player wins the whole pot. Everyone puts in another piece.

ה Hay: Player wins half the pot.

פ Pey: Player puts one piece of gelt in the pot.

When all your gelt is gone, you're out.

The Dreidel Game

All players put one piece of gelt into the middle, "the pot". Players take turns spinning the dreidel:

נ Nun: Player wins nothing.

ג Gimmel: Player wins the whole pot. Everyone puts in another piece.

ה Hay: Player wins half the pot.

פ Pey: Player puts one piece of gelt in the pot.

When all your gelt is gone, you're out.

The Dreidel Game

All players put one piece of gelt into the middle, "the pot". Players take turns spinning the dreidel:

נ Nun: Player wins nothing.

ג Gimmel: Player wins the whole pot. Everyone puts in another piece.

ה Hay: Player wins half the pot.

פ Pey: Player puts one piece of gelt in the pot.

When all your gelt is gone, you're out.

The Dreidel Game

All players put one piece of gelt into the middle, "the pot". Players take turns spinning the dreidel:

נ Nun: Player wins nothing.

ג Gimmel: Player wins the whole pot. Everyone puts in another piece.

ה Hay: Player wins half the pot.

פ Pey: Player puts one piece of gelt in the pot.

When all your gelt is gone, you're out.

The Dreidel Game

All players put one piece of gelt into the middle, "the pot". Players take turns spinning the dreidel:

נ Nun: Player wins nothing.

ג Gimmel: Player wins the whole pot. Everyone puts in another piece.

ה Hay: Player wins half the pot.

פ Pey: Player puts one piece of gelt in the pot.

When all your gelt is gone, you're out.

The Dreidel Game

All players put one piece of gelt into the middle, "the pot". Players take turns spinning the dreidel:

נ Nun: Player wins nothing.

ג Gimmel: Player wins the whole pot. Everyone puts in another piece.

ה Hay: Player wins half the pot.

פ Pey: Player puts one piece of gelt in the pot.

When all your gelt is gone, you're out.

The Dreidel Game

All players put one piece of gelt into the middle, "the pot". Players take turns spinning the dreidel:

נ Nun: Player wins nothing.

ג Gimmel: Player wins the whole pot. Everyone puts in another piece.

ה Hay: Player wins half the pot.

פ Pey: Player puts one piece of gelt in the pot.

When all your gelt is gone, you're out.

The Dreidel Game

All players put one piece of gelt into the middle, "the pot". Players take turns spinning the dreidel:

נ Nun: Player wins nothing.

ג Gimmel: Player wins the whole pot. Everyone puts in another piece.

ה Hay: Player wins half the pot.

פ Pey: Player puts one piece of gelt in the pot.

When all your gelt is gone, you're out.

The Dreidel Game

All players put one piece of gelt into the middle, "the pot". Players take turns spinning the dreidel:

נ Nun: Player wins nothing.

ג Gimmel: Player wins the whole pot. Everyone puts in another piece.

ה Hay: Player wins half the pot.

פ Pey: Player puts one piece of gelt in the pot.

When all your gelt is gone, you're out.

The Dreidel Game

All players put one piece of gelt into the middle, "the pot". Players take turns spinning the dreidel:

נ Nun: Player wins nothing.

ג Gimmel: Player wins the whole pot. Everyone puts in another piece.

ה Hay: Player wins half the pot.

פ Pey: Player puts one piece of gelt in the pot.

When all your gelt is gone, you're out.

The Dreidel Game

All players put one piece of gelt into the middle, "the pot". Players take turns spinning the dreidel:

נ Nun: Player wins nothing.

ג Gimmel: Player wins the whole pot. Everyone puts in another piece.

ה Hay: Player wins half the pot.

פ Pey: Player puts one piece of gelt in the pot.

When all your gelt is gone, you're out.

The Dreidel Game

All players put one piece of gelt into the middle, "the pot". Players take turns spinning the dreidel:

נ Nun: Player wins nothing.

ג Gimmel: Player wins the whole pot. Everyone puts in another piece.

ה Hay: Player wins half the pot.

פ Pey: Player puts one piece of gelt in the pot.

When all your gelt is gone, you're out.

Sew Jewish

Purim Mishloach Manot Boxes

...the city of Shushan rang with joyous cries. The Jews enjoyed light and gladness, happiness and honor. (Esther 8:15-16)

On Purim we celebrate Queen Esther saving the Jews of ancient Persia, including its capital city of Shushan, from a plot by the evil courtier Haman. One way we celebrate is by giving gifts of food and drink, called mishloach manot—also known by the slightly easier to pronounce variation, "shalach manot." Your friends and family will love receiving mishloach manot in these festive boxes. After you fill them with tasty foods—according to a widely-followed teaching, at least two different foods that are ready to eat—wrap them in cellophane and ribbon. After the holiday, the boxes become handy catch-all organizers on a desk, side table, or countertop. Many people follow the tradition of giving mishloach manot to at least two people on Purim, so the fabric yardages in the materials list provide enough fabric for two boxes.

Finished size: 6¼" x 3¾" (15.9cm x 9.5cm)

Materials

Recommended fabrics: Heavy-weight cotton home decorating fabrics, especially canvas and duck

Fabric for two boxes:

Box: 1/2 yd. (40 cm) at least 44" (112cm) wide **OR** 3/8 yd. (40cm) at least 54" (137cm) wide

Lining: 1/2 yd. (40cm) at least 44" (112cm) wide **OR** 3/8 yd. (40cm) at least 54" wide (137cm) wide

Iron-on craft backing: 7/8 yd. (80cm) at least 20" (51cm) wide

Thread

 Tip: When choosing your lining fabric, avoid patterns that run in only one direction. Otherwise, when you fold the top of the box over in the final step, the lining pattern will appear upside down on the outside of the boxes.

Special Equipment

Transfer paper

Instructions

Copy the Pattern

Copy or trace the pages for the side pattern and tape them together using the guidelines (for tips, see Basic Techniques: Copying and Tracing Patterns on page 137).

Make two copies of the base pattern and tape them together along the guidelines to make a circle.

Cut the Fabric

Cut two copies each of the side pattern and the base pattern from both the box fabric and the lining. Use the diagrams below for help fitting all the pieces on the fabric, depending on the fabric width.

44" (112cm) Wide

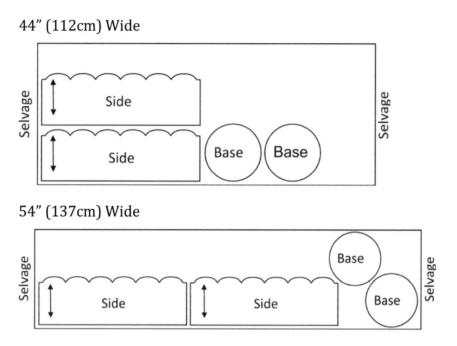

54" (137cm) Wide

Use the transfer paper to transfer the dots on the pattern to the wrong sides of all of the lining side pieces (see Basic Techniques: Transferring Pattern Markings on page 139).

Sew Basting Stitches

Baste along the long, straight edge of all the side pieces, ½" (1.2cm) from the edge. Baste around all the base pieces, ½" (1.2cm) from the edge.

Affix the Craft Backing

Note: From this point on, the sewing instructions describe making one box. Sew the second box the same way.

Cut one copy of the side pattern and one copy of the base pattern from the craft backing. Trim ½" (1.2cm) from around the outer edge of the base piece.

Position the craft backing on the wrong side of the box fabric pieces, making sure that the fusible side of the backing faces the fabric. Affix the backing to the fabric using an iron and following the manufacturer's instructions.

 Tip: Before you iron the craft backing to the fabric, double check that the fusible side of the backing faces the fabric. If the fusible side is up, the backing will end up sticking to your iron.

Sew the Side Pieces

Note: The backing won't be shown in the diagrams that follow.

Start with the side piece cut from the box fabric: With right sides together, sew the short edges together to form a tube. Trim the seam allowance to ¼" (6mm) and press it open.

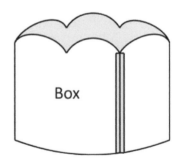

Now the lining: With right sides together, sew the short edges together, leaving the seam allowance open between the small dots. Unlike the box, don't trim the seam allowance. Press the seam allowance open.

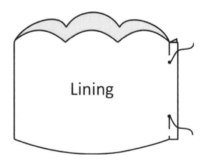

Place the box side inside the lining side, with right sides of the fabric together and matching the seams. Pin the pieces together along the scalloped edge. Sew ¼" (6mm) from the scalloped edge, pivoting at the dots. Clip the seam allowance close to the stitches at the pivot points and along the curves.

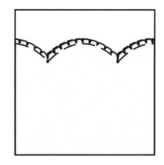

 Tip: Notice we're using a ¼" (6mm) seam allowance here, unlike the ½" (1.2cm) seam allowance used for most of the project.

Topstitch the Scalloped Edge

Turn the fabrics right side out, opening the scalloped edge fully to the seam. Press. With the lining facing up, topstitch 1/8" (3mm) along the scalloped edge.

Attach the Base Pieces

Pull the layers of fabric apart to make one long tube with the wrong sides of the fabrics facing out.

With right sides together, pin the box base to the unfinished edge of the box side, matching the basting stitches. With the base facing up on your sewing machine, sew the pieces together ½" (1.2cm) from the edge. Trim the seam allowance to ¼" (6mm).

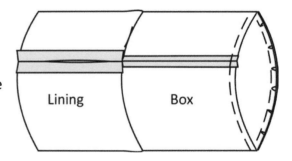

Sew the lining base to the lining side in the same way.

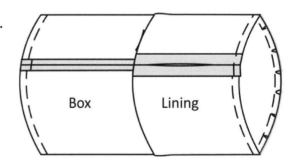

Close the Lining

Turn the box right side out by pulling the fabric through the opening in the lining. Open the fabric out fully along the seam lines. Press along the base seam lines.

Fold the lining along the side seam and pin the layers of fabric together along the opening, matching the pressed edges. Sew along the opening 1/8" (3mm) from the edge.

Push the lining to the inside of the box.

Finish

Fold the side down toward the outside of the box so that the box is about 3¾" (9cm) high.

Pattern

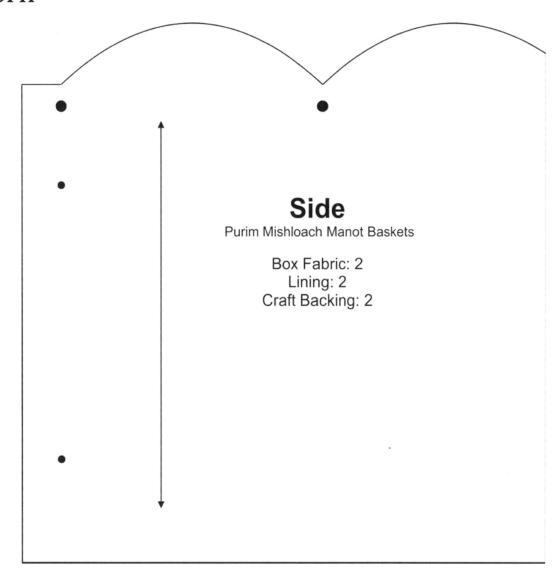

Side

Purim Mishloach Manot Baskets

Box Fabric: 2
Lining: 2
Craft Backing: 2

The completed pattern looks like this:

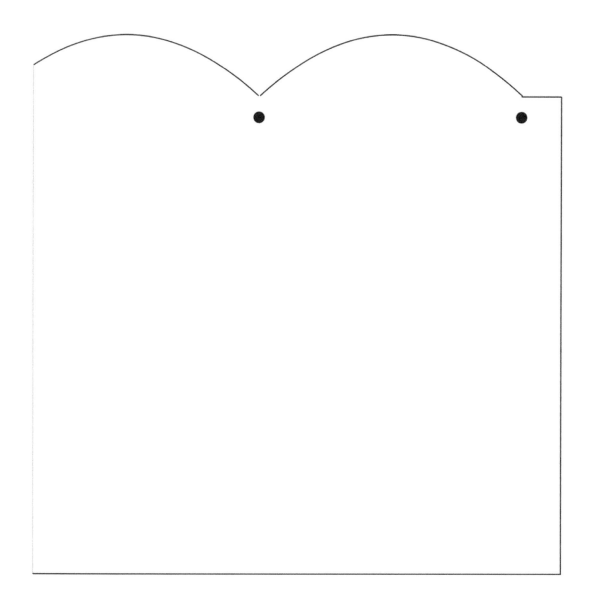

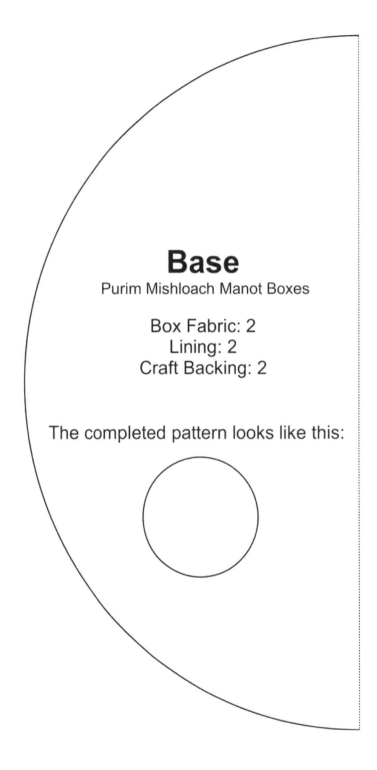

Base

Purim Mishloach Manot Boxes

Box Fabric: 2
Lining: 2
Craft Backing: 2

The completed pattern looks like this:

Passover Matzah Cover

This is the bread of affliction, which our ancestors ate in the land of Egypt.—The Passover Haggadah

Matzah is one of the central elements of the Passover Seder, when we celebrate the Israelites' redemption from slavery in ancient Egypt. We eat matzah to remember that the Israelites left Egypt in such a hurry that they didn't have time to let their bread dough rise. This matzah cover, with its chirping bird and new leaves, will bring a cheerful spring feel to your Passover Seder table. The letters spell *"Pesach,"* the Hebrew word for the holiday. The cover has three pockets—one for each piece of matzah used during the Seder.

Back view.

Finished size: 11¼" x 11¼" (28.6cm x 28.6cm)

Materials

Recommended fabrics: Medium weight linen, cotton, cotton blends

Fabric:

Cover and Pockets: 3/8 yd. (30cm) at least 45" (115cm) wide

Border/Appliques: 3/8 yd. (30cm) at least 45" (115cm) wide

Iron-on adhesive web

Thread

Embroidery floss, cotton or polyester

Special Equipment

Transfer paper

Water or air erasable fabric marker

Embroidery needle, size 5-10

Small embroidery hoop

 Tip: The materials list calls for linen or cotton fabric, but you could also use silk or silk-like fabrics. If you do, use fusible tricot interfacing instead of iron-on adhesive web, and follow the instructions in Basic Techniques: Making Appliques from Silk and Silk-like Fabrics on page 141.

Instructions

Copy the Pattern

Copy or trace the pattern pages for the border and cover patterns and tape them together using the guidelines (for tips, see Basic Techniques: Copying and Tracing Patterns on page 137).

Cut the Fabric

Cover and Pockets Fabric: Cut four copies of the cover and pockets pattern. Use the transfer paper to transfer the dots to the right side of all four pieces.

Border/Applique Fabric: Cut four copies of the border pattern, reserving a section of fabric for the appliques. Transfer the dots to the wrong side of all the fabric pieces.

Finish the Edges of the Squares

Use close zigzag stitches to finish the edges of the four fabric squares.

Make the Appliques

On one of the squares, use the erasable fabric marker to trace the applique and embroidery guidelines onto the right side of the fabric.

 Tip: The square with the applique and embroidery guidelines will become the cover, and the other three squares will become the pockets for the matzah.

Copy the applique patterns.

Create appliques for the letters and bird using the applique patterns, the reserved border fabric, and the adhesive web (see Basic Techniques: Machine Applique, Making Appliques from Cotton and Linen Fabrics on page 140). Remove the backing from the adhesive web, position the appliques onto the cover, and iron them into place using the instructions provided by the adhesive web's manufacturer.

Finish the Appliques

Finish the edges of the appliques with close, medium width zigzag stitches (see Basic Techniques: Machine Applique, Finishing Machine Appliques on page 142).

Embroider the Leaves

Embroider the leaves using the backstitch and a double strand of floss (see Basic Techniques: Hand Embroidery on page 144).

Make the Border

Note: Use a ½" (1.2cm) seam allowance throughout.

With right sides together, sew two border pieces together along one pointed end, between the dots.

Clip the corners and grade the seam allowance.

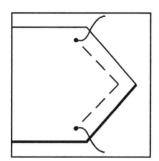

Use the same technique to sew all four border pieces together end to end to make a frame.

Press the seams open. If you find it difficult to press the seams open all the way to the corner, try to press to at least ½" (1cm) from the corner.

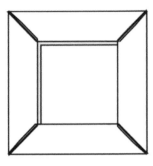

Attach the Border to the Cover

Pin one unfinished edge of the border to one edge of the cover, with the right side of the border facing the wrong side of the cover, and matching edges and dots. Make sure the seam allowances lie flat. Sew between the dots.

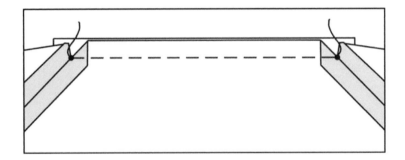

Sew the remaining border pieces to the other three edges of the cover one side at a time, each time matching edges and dots.

Press the seam allowances toward the border.

Press under the freeedges of the border pieces ½" (1.2 cm) from the edge.

Turn the pressed edges of the border to the front of the cover so that they just cover the stitches. Pin the border in place.

Sew only the bottom border to the cover, sewing close to the inner pressed edge.

Sew Jewish

Add the Pockets

Stack the three remaining fabric squares on top of each other, right sides up and matching the edges and dots. Center the stack under the cover, matching dots. Pin.

Sew along the top and side sections of the border close to the inner pressed edge, sewing through all thicknesses of fabric. Avoid sewing the bottom edge to keep the pockets open on that side.

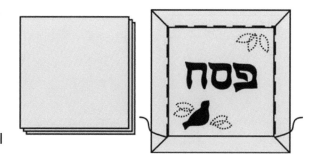

Pattern

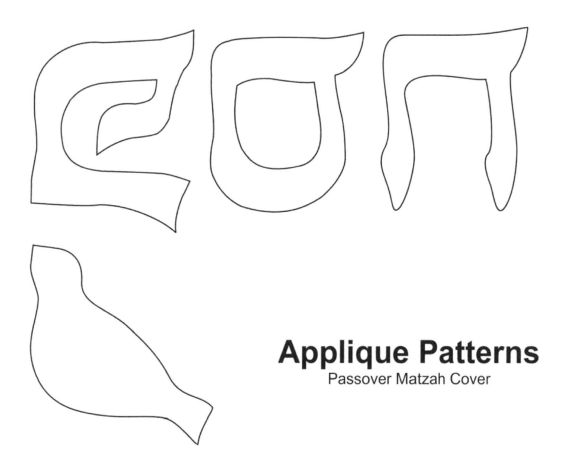

Applique Patterns
Passover Matzah Cover

Cover and Pockets

Passover Matzah Cover

Cut 4 from Fabric

The completed
cover and pockets
pattern looks like this:

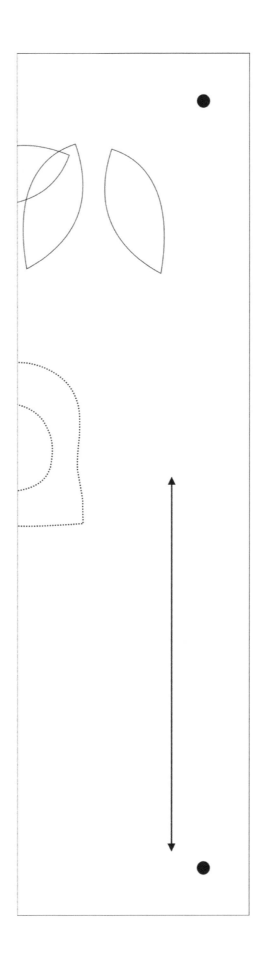

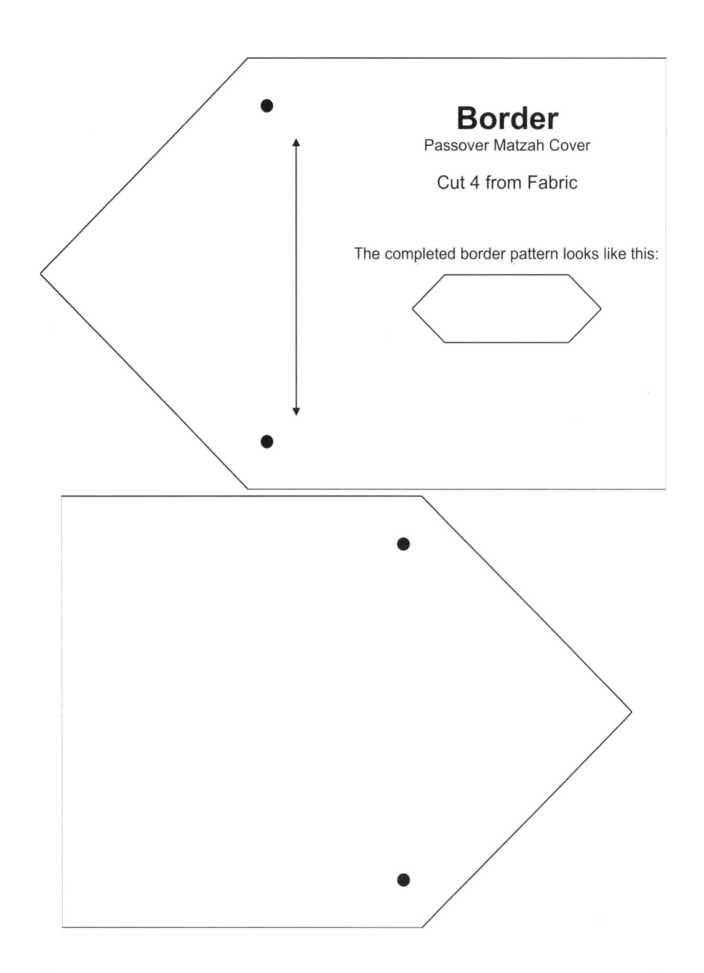

Border
Passover Matzah Cover

Cut 4 from Fabric

The completed border pattern looks like this:

Hand Washing Towel

Blessed are you, Lord our God, Ruler of the universe, who has sanctified us with Your commandments and commanded us concerning the washing of hands.—Blessing for washing hands

The ritual hand washing before eating bread or bread products is no ordinary hand washing, so why use an ordinary towel to dry your hands? This towel has high-quality details: a mitered hem and wave tucks that suggest flowing water. We're making it with linen, so you'll love the feel of it in your hands, especially as it softens over time.

Finished size: 14½" x 21" (36.8cm x 53.3cm)

Materials

Fabric: White linen, 5/8 yd. (60cm) at least 35" (90cm) wide
Thread

 Tip: We're going to shrink the linen as part of the project, so you can buy the amount specified here without adding extra fabric.

Special Equipment

Pattern paper (For alternatives see Basic Techniques: Making Patterns on page 138.)
Water or air erasable fabric marker

Instructions

Shrink the Linen

Wash the fabric in hot water with a little mild soap. Dry it using a high setting, and remove it promptly. Iron it to remove any wrinkles.

 Tip: Avoid twisting the linen when it's wet since this can create permanent wrinkles.

Make the Pattern

Use the pattern paper to make a rectangular pattern 17" x 27 ¼" (43cm x 69cm).

Cut the Fabric

Cut one copy of the pattern from the linen.

Mark the Sewing Guidelines

Copy or trace the pages of the sewing guidelines pattern , and tape the pages together using the guidelines (for tips, see Basic Techniques: Copying and Tracing Patterns on page 137).

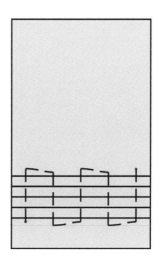

Use the erasable fabric marker to trace the sewing guidelines onto the right side of the fabric and to mark the positions of the dots (see Basic Techniques: Transferring Pattern Markings on page 139). The bottom fold line should be 3 5/8" (9cm) away from the bottom edge of the towel. Use a yard stick or other straight edge as you trace the fold lines to help keep them straight.

Sew the Tucks

Fold along the fold line closest to the bottom of the towel with the right side of the fabric on the outside of the fold. Press. Sew across the towel 3/8" (1 cm) from the pressed edge.

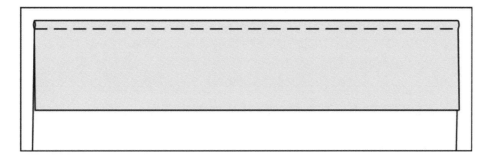

 Tip: To create the best effect, take the time to place the folds and stitches accurately.

Fold along the second fold line, and with the first tuck facing up on the ironing board to help keep it out of the way, press.

Sew 3/8" (1 cm) from the pressed edge.

 Tip: Keep the finished tuck facing up on your machine to keep it out of the way as you sew the next tuck.

Finish the remaining three tucks in the same way.

Make Some Waves

Press the tucks alternately up and down along the wave sewing line and pin them to the towel as shown in the diagram. Keep the pins parallel to the wave sewing line with their heads oriented toward the pressed edge of the pleat so that you can pull them out easily as you sew.

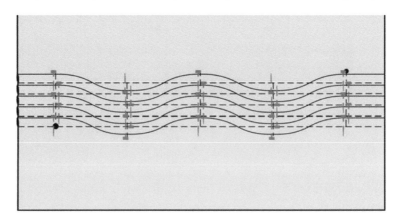

Stitch along the wave sewing line, beginning at the large dot and stopping at the small dot, removing the pins as you go.

 Tip: As you sew along the curved lines above and below the tucks, be sure to avoid sewing over the tucks. To work around them, sew a few stitches along the curved line, then, with the needle in the fabric raise the presser foot and move the tuck out of the way. Lower the presser foot and continue sewing.

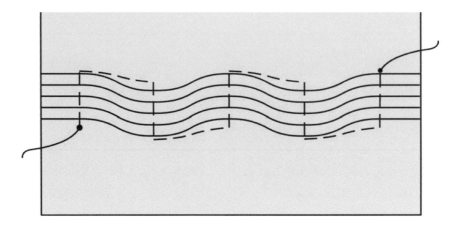

Sew the Mitered Hem

Use the erasable fabric marker to mark 1¼" (3.2cm) hemlines on all four sides of the towel.

Press the raw edges of the towel to the wrong side along the hem lines. Turn the raw edges to the inside of the hem to meet the pressed edge. Press again.

Unfold one corner. With the right side of the towel facing up on your ironing board, fold the corner toward the center of the towel, matching the hem lines on the corner to the hem lines on the towel, as in the diagram. Press along the fold.

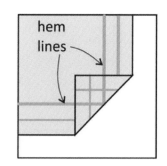

Unfold the corner again. Fold the corner along the diagonal with the right side of the fabric on the inside of the fold, matching the raw edges and the pressed diagonal line, as in the diagram.

Sew along the diagonal pressed line, beginning at the fold and stopping at the outer pressed line, as in the diagram.

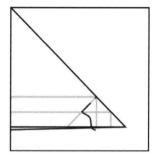

Tip: To help you easily see where to sew, draw along the sewing line with the erasable fabric marker before stitching.

Trim the seam allowance to ¼" (6mm) and clip the corner.

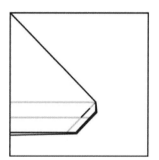

Turn the corner right side out, fully opening it to the point at the corner. Refold the hem, tucking the raw edges back inside the hem. Pin the hem in place.

Finish the remaining three corners in the same way.

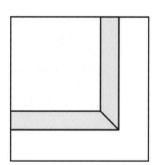

Pin the hems along all four sides. Sew around the entire hem close to the inner pressed edge.

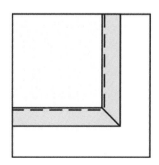

Remove the Markings

Use water to remove any remaining markings. Press the fabric between your hands to remove the excess water, but avoid twisting the fabric, which could create permanent wrinkles.

You'll notice that the area of the towel with the wave tucks will be narrower than the rest of the towel. While the towel is still wet, stretch that section to help restore the width.

Dry the towel in the dryer or let it air dry.

Iron the towel to remove any wrinkles. Avoid pressing the iron down directly on top of the wave tucks, but run the iron gently over the back of the tuck area.

Pattern

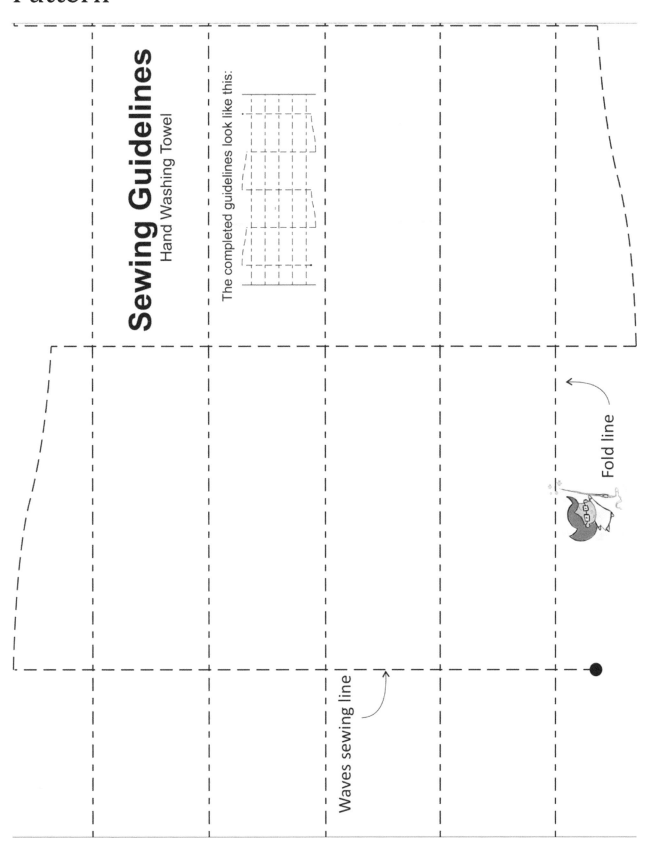

Sewing Guidelines
Hand Washing Towel

The completed guidelines look like this:

Fold line

Waves sewing line

Havdalah Spice Pouch

Blessed are you, Lord our God, Ruler of the universe, creator of various kinds of spices.—Blessing over spices

The Sages tell us that the scent of spices nourishes our soul, so they incorporated a blessing over spices into the Havdalah ritual that ends Shabbat. This little rustic bag holds a spoonful of whole cloves, with their deep, homey scent to feed your soul.

Finished size: 2-2½" (5-6.4cm) x 2 7/8" (7.3cm)

Materials

Burlap ribbon: 2½" - 3" (6.4cm – 7.6cm) wide
Thread
Twine
1 Tablespoon whole cloves

Special Equipment

Small safety pin

 Tip: You could make this pouch from organza ribbon instead of burlap. If you do, replace the twine with double-sided ribbon that is 1/8" (3cm) wide.

Instructions

Sew the Tie Casings

Cut an 8½" (22cm) length of ribbon.

Turn under 1 3/8" (3.5cm) on each end and press.

To create casings for the ties, sew across the ends of the ribbon 3/8" (1cm) and 7/8" (2cm) from each end.

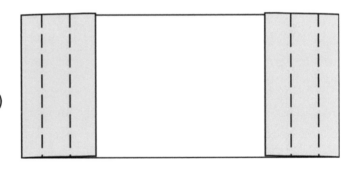

Sew the Sides

Bring the two ends of the ribbon together, and fold the ribbon in half with the right side of the ribbon on the inside of the fold.

Sew ¼" (6mm) along the sides of the pouch, leaving the area between the casing stitches open.

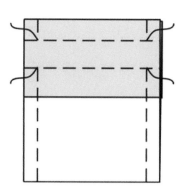

Add the Ties

Cut two 10" (25cm) lengths of twine.

Tie a knot in one piece of twine about ½" (1.2cm) from the end. Attach the safety pin to the knot by pushing the point of the pin through the knot. Close the pin. Use the head of the safety pin to thread the twine through the casing on one side of the pouch, then pass it back through the casing on the other side to where you started, keeping the trailing end from going into the casing.

Remove the safety pin, untie the knot, then knot the two ends of the twine together about ½" (1.2cm) away from the end. Use the same technique to pass the second piece of twine through the casing, this time starting on the opposite side of the pouch.

Pass the knots to the inside of the pouch through the openings in the sides, and pull the ends of the twine through to the inside.

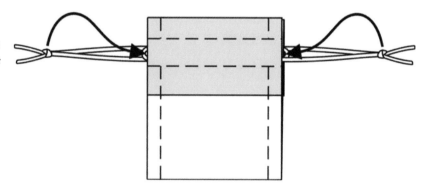

Turn the pouch right side out.

Spoon the cloves into the pouch, and pull both ties to close.

Weddings and Bar/Bat Mitzvah Celebrations

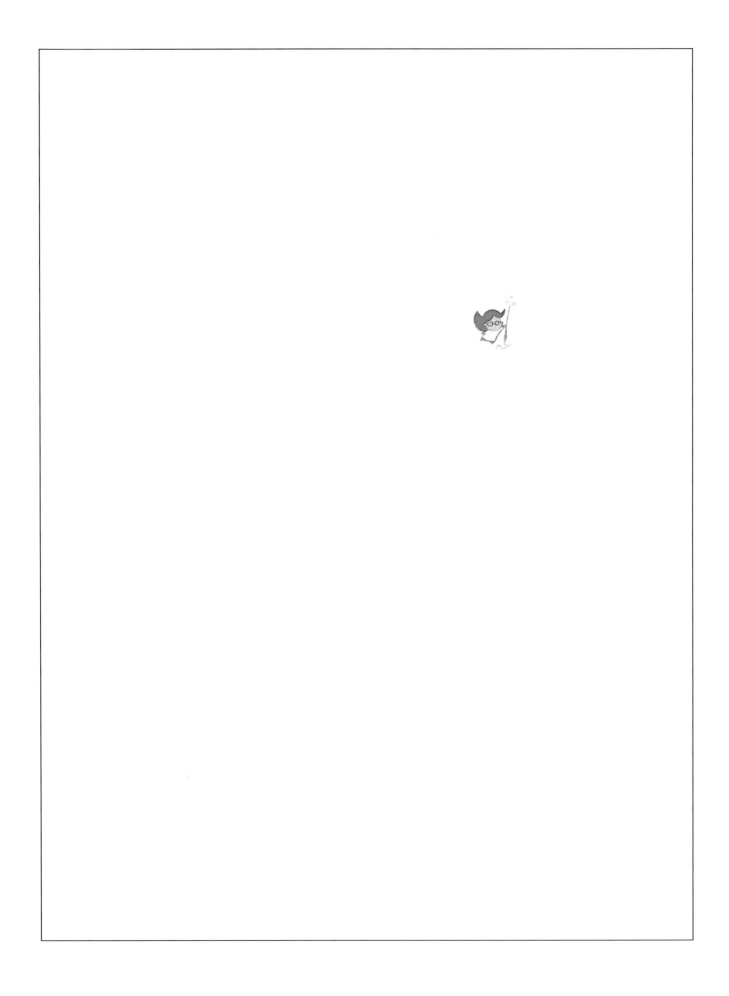

Wedding Huppah

I am my beloved's, and my beloved is mine. (Song of Songs 2:16)

The huppah symbolizes the Jewish wedding. It represents the couple's physical home as well as their shared spiritual space. At Huppahs.com, where I started offering my handmade huppahs for rent some years ago, the most popular style season after season is a simple white canopy. I'm going to show you how to make your own simple canopy with streamlined construction techniques. Like any simple design, the key to beautiful results lies in using good quality fabric. Silk, jacquard, brocade, and other woven fabrics work beautifully, but feel free to look beyond the special occasion section of your fabric shop for something that captures your own spirit. Choose a lightweight or medium weight fabric that drapes well and looks good from both sides. During the wedding, the poles can be held by four honored guests, or you can make stands to hold them, as you see in the photo. You'll find an instructional video for the stands called "DIY Wedding Chuppah Stands" on the Sew Jewish YouTube channel.

Finished size of canopy: 72" x 72" (183cm x 183cm)

Materials

Recommended fabrics: Lightweight or medium weight satin, silk, Dupioni silk, jacquard, brocade

Fabric: 5 yd. (4.6m) at least 45" (115cm) **OR** 4½ yd. (4.1m) at least 54" (137cm)
Thread
Fusible interfacing (Only needed if using lightweight fabric.)

Poles
4 Wooden poles, at least 1" (2.5cm) in diameter and 7'-8' (2.1m – 2.4m) long
4 Wooden finials
Wood glue
Paint or varnish for finishing the poles (Optional)
4 Eye screws

Special Equipment

Pattern paper (For alternatives see Basic Techniques: Making Patterns on page 138.)

Instructions

Make the Patterns

Use the pattern paper to make three pattern pieces of the following sizes:

Side: 20" x 73½" (51cm x 187cm)
Middle: 36" x 73½" (91cm x 187cm)
Tie: 2" x 20" (5cm x 51cm)

Cut the Fabric

Cut the required number of copies of each pattern. Use the diagrams on the next page for help fitting all of the pattern pieces on the fabric, whether your fabric is 45" (115cm) or 54" (137cm) wide:

45" (115cm) Wide

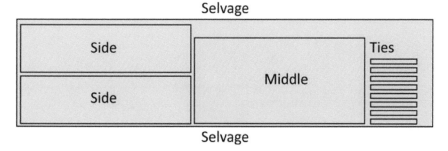

54" (137cm) Wide

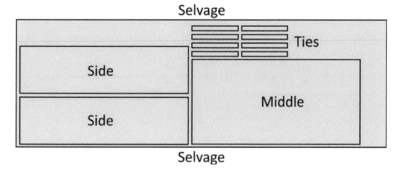

Sew the Ties

If using lightweight fabric, cut eight copies of the tie pattern from the interfacing. Fuse the interfacing to the wrong side of the ties following the manufacturer's instructions. The interfacing won't be shown on the diagrams.

For all weight fabrics, fold one tie in half lengthwise with the right side of the fabric on the inside of the fold. Fold both raw edges toward the folded edge with the wrong side of the fabric inside the folds. Press.

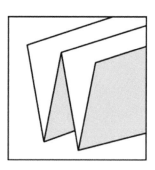

Sew across one end of the tie, ½" (1.2cm) from the end.

Turn the raw edges to the inside of the tie. Press the tie flat. Sew 1/8" (3mm) from the long open edge.

Sew the remaining seven ties in the same way.

Sew the Canopy Pieces Together

With wrong sides together, sew one side piece to the middle piece along a long edge using a ¼" (6mm) seam allowance.

 Tip: Notice that we're sewing this first seam with the wrong side of the fabrics facing each other, rather than with the right sides facing each other as with most seams, and we're using a ¼" (6mm) seam allowance rather than a ½" (1.2cm) seam allowance.

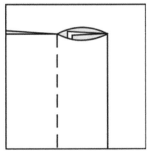

Press the seam allowance toward the middle piece. Fold the canopy along the seam line so that the right sides of the fabrics are on the inside of the fold, making sure the stitches lie right along the fold line.

Press along the fold. Sew 3/8" (1cm) from the pressed edge.

Unfold the canopy and press the seam allowance toward the middle piece. Working from the right side of the fabric, secure the seam allowance to the canopy by sewing ¼" (6mm) from the previous seam.

 Tip: As you sew, use your fingertips to gently pull the middle and side pieces away from each other so that the middle piece lies flat over the seam allowance beneath.

Sew the second side piece to the other long edge of the middle piece using the same technique.

Prepare the Hems and Corners

Baste around the entire canopy, 5/8" (1.5cm) from the edge.

Turn the edges of the canopy to the wrong side along the basting stitches and press. Turn under another 5/8" (1.5cm) and press again. Pin the pressed edges to hold them in place while you work on the next steps.

Unfold one corner. Fold the corner to the wrong side so that the tip meets the inner fold. Fold in again and press.

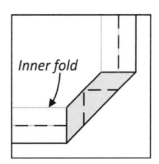

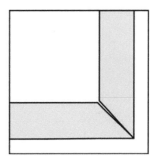

With the corner still folded in, refold the edges of the canopy along the previous fold lines to form the hem. Press and pin.

Prepare the remaining three corners in the same way.

Attach the Ties and Finish the Hems

We're going to finish the hem on one side of the canopy at a time. At one corner, remove the pins from a 10" (25cm) length of the folded edge. Insert a tie halfway (9" or 23cm) into the inside of the folded hem with the unfinished end of the tie inside the hem. Pin in place.

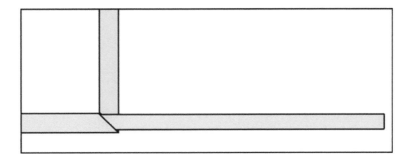

Insert another tie into the opposite corner of the same side of the canopy. Pin the hem in place.

Sew around the interior of the entire folded area of the hem, 1/8" (3mm) from the folded edges. Be sure to sew through the ties to secure them to the canopy.

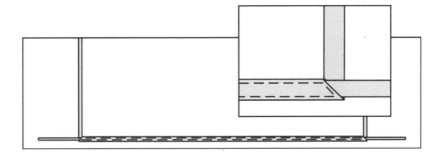

Finish the remaining three sides of the canopy in the same way.

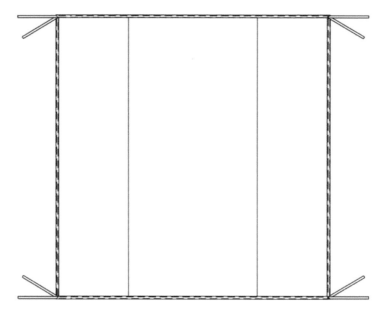

Make the Poles

Screw the eye screws into the poles about 1" (2.5cm) from the tops of each pole.

Use the wood glue to attach the finials to the tops of the poles. Allow the glue to dry.

If you plan to finish the poles with paint or varnish, do that now.

Tie the Canopy to the Poles

For each corner of the canopy, pass one of the two ties through the eye screw. Hold the ties together close to the screw and knot them together, moving the knot close to the screw as you tighten it.

Store the huppah with the canopy untied from the poles.

 Tip: Store wooden poles horizontally or vertically straight to avoid the natural bending that occurs in wood over time.

Sew Jewish

Bridal Veil

Your eyes are like doves' behind your veil. (Song of Songs 4:1)

The veil is so important in a traditional Jewish wedding that it has its own ceremony, the bedeken, before the huppah ceremony, when the groom lowers the veil over the bride's face. If you're thinking of doing any wedding DIY, start with the veil. A simple, classic drop veil is easy to make by machine or by hand, and after the wedding you'll have an especially personal keepsake. This drop veil has a circular shape. The instructions will show you how to customize the size. We're going to edge the veil in scalloped lace trim not only because it's lovely, but also because it's easy to work with. It's wide enough to allow you to be less than razor precise when placing the lace on the veil's edge, and the scalloped shape helps the lace lie flat along the veil's curves for a look that's simply beautiful.

Finished size: Customized

Materials

Recommended fabrics: Tulle, Illusion

Fabric: See the first step of the instructions to determine the width and yardage.

Scalloped lace trim, finished on both edges: See the second step of the instructions to determine the length required.

Thread

Special Equipment

Tape measure

String

Pattern paper (For alternatives see Basic Techniques: Making Patterns on page 138.)

Hand-sewing needle, size 6-8 (Optional. Only needed if you are going to attach the lace by hand.)

Instructions

Determine the Length of the Veil

From the top of your head, measure how long you'd like the veil to drape in the front and back. Classic lengths are to the shoulder (or just below the shoulder), elbow, or fingertips.

Add the front and back drapes together to determine the diameter of the veil. If you'll be wearing your hair in a bun or another hair style with a lot of volume, add two to three more inches.

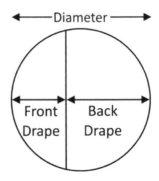

 Tip: To help get an accurate measurement, have a second person do the measuring. Be sure to stand up straight!

You'll need a piece of fabric that is at least as wide and as long as the diameter of the veil.

 Tip: Most veil fabrics are 54" to 72" (137cm to 180cm) wide, but you'll find some as wide as 108" (280cm).

Determine the Length of Trim Required

Multiply the veil's diameter by 3.2. Add 12" (25cm) more to determine the length of trim required.

Make the Pattern

Use the pattern paper to make a square pattern with sides equal to half the veil's diameter.

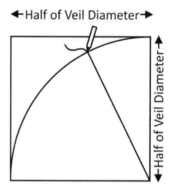

Now we're going to draw an arc across the pattern. Anchor a string at one corner of the pattern. Extend the other end of the string to an adjoining corner, and mark the length on the string. Sweep the free end of the string across the pattern to the opposite corner, drawing the position of the mark on the string onto the pattern with a pencil as you go.

Cut the Fabric

Fold the fabric into quarters. Place the pattern on the folded fabric, matching the folded edges of the fabric with the sides of the pattern that are inside the arc. Pin in place. Cut along the arc. Unfold the veil.

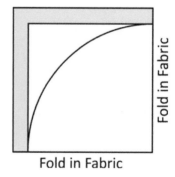

 Tip: Before you cut the fabric, double check that the folds of the fabric are under the sides of the pattern that are inside the arc. Otherwise, you won't create a circle.

Add the Trim

With the wrong side of the trim facing the right side of the veil, and with the trim overhanging the edge of the veil slightly, sew the trim to the veil by machine or by hand. If you use a machine, use a zigzag stitch with a narrow width and long stitch length. If you sew by hand, use running stitches, adjusting the stitch length as necessary so that the stitches blend in to the lace (see Basic Techniques: Hand Sewing on page 147).

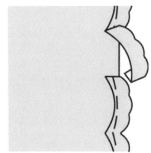

 Tip: To hide the ends of the threads, begin and end each new length of thread by passing the needle between the veil and lace, and trim the ends close to the lace.

Kippah

Know before Whom you stand. (Berachot 28b)

The custom of covering one's head with a kippah, especially during prayer, is considered a sign of reverence before God. You might know the kippah by its other name: yarmulke. There are lots of kippah styles in the world, and this one is a classic for special occasions. Make one in white for a wedding or a colorful fabric for a bar or bat mitzvah celebration. The design sits closer to the head than most commercially available satin kippahs for a more refined look. This style is usually made of satin, but you can use just about any medium weight fabric that suits the occasion and your personal style.

Finished size: 6¼" (15.9cm) diameter

Materials

Recommended fabrics: Medium weight woven fabrics, especially satin, but also jacquard, Dupioni silk, brocade, velvet, cotton

Fabric:

Kippah: ¼ yd. (20cm) at least 35" (90cm) wide

Lining: ¼ yd. (20cm) at least 35" (90cm) wide

Light-weight fusible polyester stiffener: ¼ yd. (20cm) at least 35" (90cm) wide (For velvet and other fabrics that can't be ironed, use heavy weight sew-in interfacing.)

Thread

 Tip: If you use a medium weight fabric other than velvet, you can use the same fabric for both the outer kippah and the lining. In that case, 3/8 yard (40cm) of fabric is enough to make both layers.

Instructions

Copy the Pattern

Copy or trace the kippah pattern (for tips, see Basic Techniques: Copying and Tracing Patterns on page 137).

 Tip: The pattern will make a kippah with a diameter of 6¼"(16cm). You can change the size by copying or scanning the pattern and adjusting the size of the printout. Just keep in mind that a small change in the pattern size will make a big change in the size of the kippah since we're repeating the pattern piece six times.

Cut the Fabric

Cut six copies each of the pattern from the kippah fabric, the lining, and the stiffener (18 pieces total).

Apply the Stiffener

Fuse the stiffener pieces to the wrong side of the kippah pieces using the manufacturer's instructions. Before ironing, make sure the rough side of the stiffening faces the wrong side of the fabric.

 Tip: If you are using velvet or another fabric that can't be ironed, use the following technique for the interfacing: Trim ¼" (6mm) from all sides of the interfacing pieces. Pin the interfacing pieces to the middle of the wrong side of the kippah pieces. Baste the interfacing to the kippah pieces, 3/8" (a little less than 1cm) from the edges.

Sew the Outer Kippah

Note: Use a ½" (1.2cm) seam allowance except where noted. The stiffener or interfacing won't be shown in the illustrations.

With right sides together and matching the notches, sew two kippah pieces together along one notched edge.

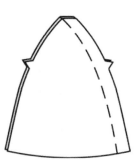

Trim the seam allowance to ¼" (6mm) and press it to one side.

 Tip: If you're using velvet or another fabric that can't be ironed, use your fingertips instead of an iron to press the fabric.

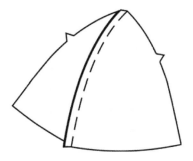

Pin a third kippah piece to an unfinished notched edge of the two attached pieces, with right sides together and matching notches. Sew along the notched edge.

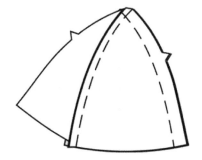

Trim the seam allowance to ¼" (6mm) and press it to one side.

Sew the other three kippah pieces together in the same way.

Sew the Two Halves Together

With right sides together, pin the two halves of the kippah together, matching the notches. Stitch from the center of the notched edge toward one end, then stitch from the center to the other end. Trim the seam allowance to ¼" (6mm).

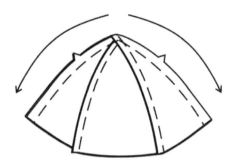

Grade the layers of fabric in the middle of the seam to reduce the bulk (see Basic Techniques: Sewing, Grade the Seam Allowance on page 147). Press the seam allowance to one side.

Sew the Lining

Sew the six lining pieces together in the same way as for the kippah pieces.

Put It All Together

With the right sides together, sew the lining to the kippah along the raw edge, leaving a 1" (2.5cm) opening.

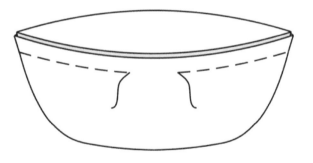

Turn the kippah right side out through the opening, turning it out fully along the seam that connects the lining to the outer kippah. Press along the seam, turning in a 1/2" (1.2cm) seam allowance at the opening. Pin the opening.

Sew around the entire kippah close to the outer edge.

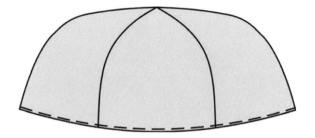

Pattern

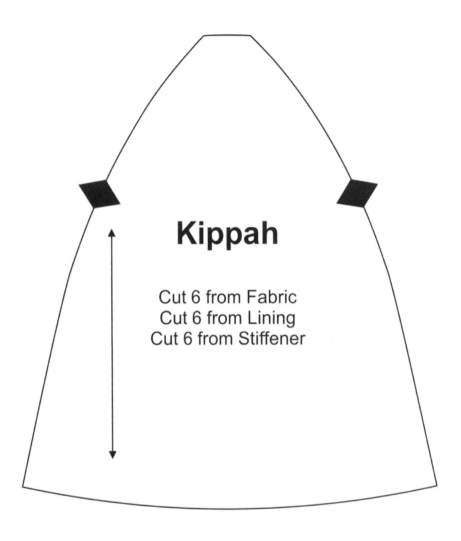

Kippah

Cut 6 from Fabric
Cut 6 from Lining
Cut 6 from Stiffener

Tallit

You shall make tassels on the four corners of the garment with which you cover yourself. (Deuteronomy 22:12)

Of all the projects in this book, the tallit is special because making a tallit involves performing a Biblical commandment—a mitzvah—the commandment to make tassels on the corners of four-cornered garments (Numbers 15:38 and Deuteronomy 22:12). Even if you have no plans to wear a tallit yourself, by making one—specifically, by tying the tzitzit strings on the corners—you perform a mitzvah. Traditionally, a young person first wears a tallit when they become a bar mitzvah, which means "son of the commandment," or a bat mitzvah, which means "daughter of the commandment." This project is a shawl-style tallit, the kind worn around the neck like a scarf, which is popular in many Jewish communities today. In other communities, as through most of Jewish history, the custom is to wear a tallit that is large enough to wrap around one's body. To make a large tallit, start with a larger piece of fabric and follow the adjustments given in the instructions.

Finished size: 64" x 18" (1.6m x 45.7cm)

Basic Anatomy of a Tallit

Before we start sewing, let's take a look at the parts of a tallit:

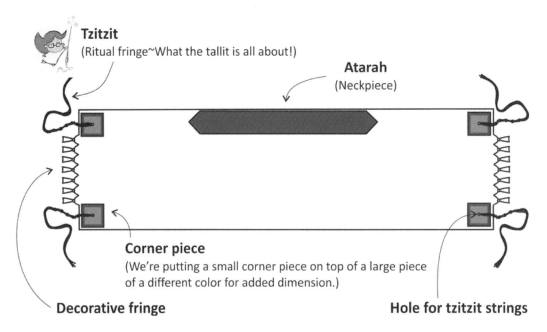

Tzitzit
(Ritual fringe~What the tallit is all about!)

Atarah
(Neckpiece)

Corner piece
(We're putting a small corner piece on top of a large piece of a different color for added dimension.)

Decorative fringe

Hole for tzitzit strings

A rich history of Jewish law and tradition lies behind every detail of the tallit—far more than I could ever include in these instructions—so I've provided a list of tallit information sources at the end of the book (page 149).

Materials

Recommended fabrics: ***Tallit:*** *Heavy-weight woven fabrics with coarse fibers including wool suiting, heavy-weight silk, polyester broadcloth (avoid linen);* ***Atarah and corner pieces:*** *Silk, silk-like fabrics, jacquard, brocade, poly satin*

Fabric:
>**Tallit:** 2 yd. (1.9m) at least 35" (90cm) wide
>**Atarah and large corner pieces:** 3/8 yd. (30cm) at least 35" (90cm) wide **OR** ¼ yd. (20cm) at least 54" (137cm) wide
>**Small corner pieces:** 1/8 yd. (10cm) at least 35" (90cm) wide

Thread to match the tallit fabric and atarah/corner pieces (Avoid thread with linen.)
Tear-away stabilizer
Purchased tzitzit strings, available from your local Judaica store or online

Tip: Avoid making the tallit with linen fabric or thread. Most commercial tzitzit strings are made from wool, and a Biblical commandment prohibits combining linen and wool in the same garment (the combination is called shatnez, and you can find the prohibition at Deuteronomy 22:11 and Leviticus 19:19).

 Another tip: For the tallit fabric, be sure to choose a woven fabric made from coarse threads. In addition to the ritual knotted tzitzit on the corners, we're going to make decorative fringe on the ends of the tallit with threads from the fabric itself, a technique that works best with heavy, coarse fibers.

 And another tip: If you'd like to make a tallit that is large enough to wrap around the body, a typical size for this style is 4' x 6' (122cm x 183cm). It should be wide enough to fall at least to the waist, and at least 24" (61cm) wide in order to follow the strictest interpretation of Jewish law. It should be long enough to stay on the shoulders when the front corners are folded back over the shoulders. For this project, be sure to add 7" (18cm) to the desired length so you have enough fabric to make the decorative fringe.

Special Equipment

Pattern paper (For alternatives see Basic Techniques: Making Patterns on page 138.)
Transfer paper
Ruler

Instructions

Make the Tallit and Atarah Patterns

Make the Tallit Pattern
Use the pattern paper to make a rectangular pattern 71" x 18¼" (180cm x 46cm).

 Tip: We're making the pattern slightly wider than 18" (45.7cm) so that if you lose some width when you finish the edges, the tallit will still be at least 18" wide, which some sources consider the minimum width for a garment to require tzitzit.

Make the Atarah Pattern
Make an atarah pattern using the dimensions in the diagram:

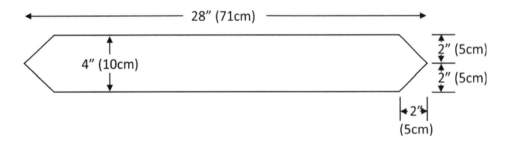

Copy the Corner Piece Patterns

Copy or trace the patterns for the large corner piece and the small corner piece. (for tips, see Basic Techniques: Copying and Tracing Patterns on page 137).

Tape the pieces of the atarah pattern together using the guidelines.

Cut the Fabric

Tallit Fabric: Place the tallit pattern on the fabric with the edge of the pattern parallel to the fabric's finished edge. Cut one copy of the tallit pattern.

Fabric for Atarah and Large Corner Pieces: Cut one copy of the atarah pattern.

Cut four copies of the large corner piece pattern. Use the transfer paper to transfer the dots from the pattern to the right side of the fabric pieces.

Fabric for the Small Corner Pieces: Cut four copies of the small corner piece pattern.

Sew Jewish

Remove a Square of Fabric at Each Corner

 Tip: In the next few steps we're going to remove a small square of fabric from each corner of the tallit. The section of fabric that remains on each end of the tallit will be turned into the decorative, non-ritual fringe.

Remove a crosswise thread 3½" (9cm) in from each end—a pin will help.

3½" (9cm)   3½" (9cm)

On the ends of the tallit, measure in 3 5/8" (9cm) from each corner, and use light pencil marks to draw lines from the edge to the removed thread. At each corner, carefully cut out the square defined by the pencil line and the removed thread.

Use the same technique to remove a square of fabric from the corners at the other end of the tallit

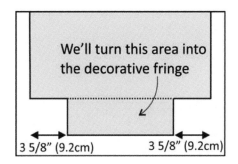

We'll turn this area into the decorative fringe

3 5/8" (9.2cm)   3 5/8" (9.2cm)

Finish the Long Edges

Finish the long edges of the tallit with medium width zigzag stitches or overlock stitches, starting and stopping about a half inch inside the fringe area.

Tip: If you'd like to try on the tallit, this is a good time to do it. Once you create the fringe in the next step you'll have a four-cornered garment, and to follow the Biblical commandment regarding tzitzit, you'll need to avoid trying on the tallit again until you've added the tzitzit.

Make the Decorative Fringes

Remove all the crosswise threads from the fringe areas. A pin can help. (This step can be a bit fiddly, but take heart – it won't take that long.)

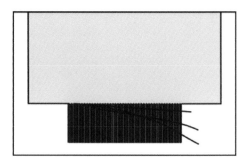

Use pins to mark off seven fringes, each a little more than 1½" (3.8cm) wide, on each end of the tallit.

 Tip: If you are making a larger tallit, mark off an odd number of fringes of equal width. There's no reason in Jewish law that the number has to be odd—an odd number of fringes just looks better than an even number.

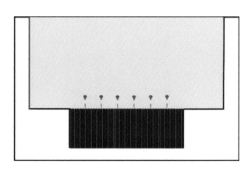

Gather the threads for each fringe, twist them together, and tie them into a knot. As you tighten each knot, make sure the tallit can lie flat, and try to position the center of the knot about 1" (2.5 cm) away from the body of the tallit.

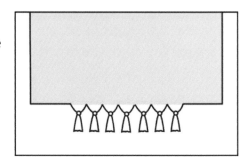

Add the Atarah

Press ½" (1.2cm) of the atarah to the wrong side along all of the edges.

Pin the atarah to the middle of one long edge of the tallit, with the wrong side of the atarah facing the right side of the tallit. (To find the middle of the atarah and tallit quickly, fold each of them in half.)

Sew around the entire atarah, 1/8" (3mm) from the edge.

 Tip: To minimize the appearance of the stitches on both sides of the tallit, match the colors of the top and bottom threads to the atarah and tallit. Do the same when you attach the corner pieces.

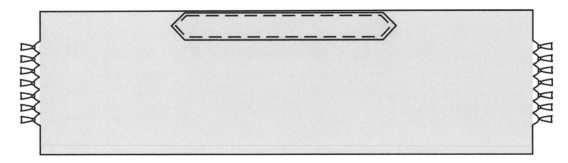

Make the Corner Pieces

For all the large and small corner pieces, press ½" (1.2cm) of fabric to the wrong side of the square along all the edges.

Pin one small corner piece to the center of a large piece, with the wrong side of the small piece facing the right side of the large piece and matching the corners of the small square to the dots on the larger piece. Sew around the entire small square, 1/8" (3mm) from the edge.

Complete the three remaining corner pieces in the same way.

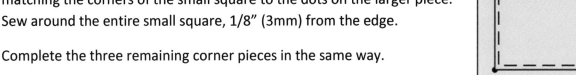

Sew the Corner Pieces to the Tallit

Pin the corner pieces to the right side of the tallit, the side with the atarah.

 Tip: If you're making a large tallit that will be folded back over the shoulders when worn, pin the corner pieces to the wrong side of the tallit, the side that doesn't have the atarah, so that they'll face outward when the tallit is worn.

Sew around the corner pieces, 1/8" (3mm) from the edges.

Make Holes for the Tzitzit Strings

Create holes for the tzitzit strings in the corner pieces using one of the following techniques:

If your machine has an eyelet or circular stitch function: Copy or trace the Tzitzit Hole Placement Guide. Use the transfer paper to transfer the circle to a corner piece. Place a piece of tear-away stabilizer under the circle area. Use your machine's eyelet or circular stitch function to sew a ¼"-diameter (6mm) circle of reinforcing stitches in the center of each corner piece, where you marked the circle. Carefully tear away the stabilizer. Use the same technique to sew holes in the remaining three corners.

OR

To sew without an eyelet or circular stitch function: Copy or trace four copies of the Tzitzit Hole Placement Guide. Place a guide on one corner piece, matching the corner and sides. Place a piece of tear-away stabilizer underneath. Sew along the center hexagon with straight stitches. Carefully tear away the placement guide from the stitches. Sew over the center of the straight stitches with narrow zigzag stitches. For the best effect, pivot at each corner when the needle is in the right-hand position of the zigzag.

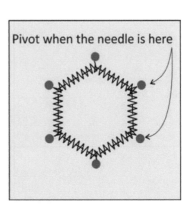

Carefully cut the fabric from inside the tzitzit hole. Avoid cutting close to the stitching.

 Tip: You don't have to cut the fabric all the way to the stitches. Once you've cut away most of the fabric from inside the tzitzit holes use the closed tip of a pair of scissors to gently push the remaining fabric fibers close to stitches.

Use the same technique to sew holes in the remaining three corners.

Affix the Tzitzit to the Corners

Note: There are several traditional patterns of knotting and twisting the tzitzit strings. These instructions will walk you through one of the most widely used. While tying the strings we recite the Hebrew phrase "L'shem mitzvah tzitzit," which means "I am doing this to fulfill the commandment of tzitzit." Some people follow the practice of reciting the phrase only when they make the first knot, as in these instructions, and some recite the phrase when they put the strings through the hole in the tallit and also each time they make a knot or wind the strings.

Gather three short tzitzit strings and one long string (the shamash). Hold them together at one end, with all the ends even with each other (at the other end of the strings the shamash will be longer).

Thread the four strands together through the hole in one corner of the tallit. Using a bobby pin like a needle can make this easier.

Pull the threads through so that all the ends of the shorter strands are about even with each other. One end of the shamash will hang lower.

You now have two sets of strings, each with four strands—one set with all the ends even, and another set with the shamash hanging lower. Keep these two sets separate while you work.

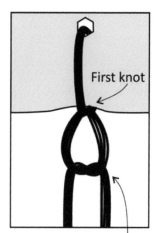

With the strings hanging from the shorter side of the tallit, tie the two sets of strings together into a knot while reciting *"L'shem mitzvah tzitzit."* Secure the knot against the fabric, crunching the fabric just slightly. Crunching the fabric in this way will help keep the tzitzit hanging from the shorter side of the tallit.

First knot

Tie a second knot close to the first.

Tighten to make the second knot.

Tip: Ideally, at the end of all the knotting and winding you'll end up with all eight ends of the strings approximately even with each other, although this isn't a requirement. To help keep the length of all the strings about the same in the finished tassel, begin tying the first knot with one set of strings, and begin the second knot with the other set of strings.

Hold all the strings except the shamash together. Wind the shamash around the other strings seven times.

Make a double knot.

Wind the shamash around the other strings eight times.

Make a double knot.

 Tip: As you work, try to keep the distance between each set of double knots the same even though the number of windings differs. It's not a requirement, just an ideal to aim for.

Wind the shamash eleven times.

Make a double knot.

Wind the shamash thirteen times.

Make a double knot.

Use the same method to affix tzitzit to the remaining three corners of the tallit.

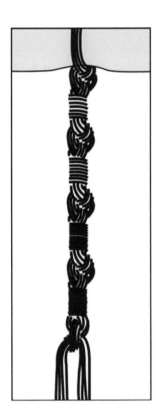

Pattern

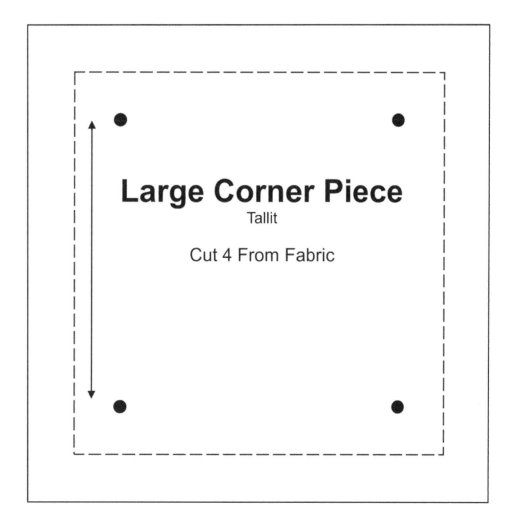

Large Corner Piece

Tallit

Cut 4 From Fabric

Small Corner Piece
Tallit

Cut 4 From Fabric

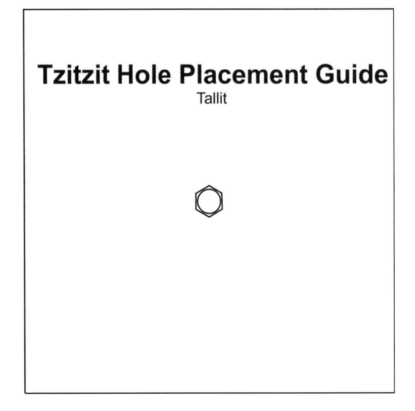

Tzitzit Hole Placement Guide
Tallit

Tallit Bag

These shall be your tassels, and when you see them, you shall remember all God's commandments so as to keep them. (Numbers 15:39)

If you're making a tallit, you'll want to make a bag to carry it. Choose a hard-wearing fabric like velvet or canvas that will stand up to years of use. The bag in the photo was made with traditional velvet, then lined with a surprise splash of modern color. It's large enough to hold the tallit as well as the tefillin in its tefillin bag, the next project in the book.

Finished size: 14¼" x 11¼" (36.2cm x 28.6cm)

Materials

Recommended fabrics: **Bag:** *Medium or heavy weight woven fabric such as velvet, canvas, twill, duck;* **Lining:** *Medium or heavy weight satin, cotton, or cotton blends*

Fabric:
> **Bag:** 3/8 yd. (30cm) at least 35" (90cm) wide
> **Lining:** 3/8 yd. (30cm) at least 35" (90cm) wide

14" (36cm) zipper
Thread

 Tip: When buying fabric, you might want to get enough to make a matching tefillin bag, the next project in the book. The instructions for both bags call for 3/8-yard (30cm) lengths of fabric, but if your fabric and lining are at least 54" (137cm) wide, then 3/8 yard (30cm) of each will be enough to make both bags. If the fabrics are narrower than 54" (137cm), you'll need the full yardages listed for both projects.

Special Equipment

Pattern paper (For alternatives see Basic Techniques: Making Patterns on page 138.)
Hand sewing needle, size 6-8 (Optional, only needed if finishing the lining by hand.)

 Tip: The threads will show in the finished bag, so if your lining is a different color than the bag and you don't want contrasting threads to show against the fabric, use two different colored threads.

Instructions

Make the Pattern

Use the pattern paper to make a rectangular pattern 15" x 12" (38cm x 30cm).

Cut the Fabric

Cut two copies each of the pattern from the bag fabric and the lining.

Attach the Zipper

Note: Use your sewing machine's zipper foot.

 Tip: If you're using velvet, use plenty of pins to keep the fabrics in place.

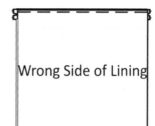

Lay one bag piece right side up on your workspace. Lay the zipper on top of the bag piece with the wrong side up and the zipper pull to the right, matching the top edges and centering the zipper horizontally (that might sound complicated, but just take a look at the illustration).

Lay a lining piece on top, wrong side up and matching the top and side edges of the fabrics. Sew ¼" (6mm) from the top edge.

 Tip: As you approach the end of the seam, stop sewing and pull the zipper tab down a few inches to get it out of the way, then finish the seam.

Lay the remaining cover piece on your work surface right side up. Position the free edge of the zipper tape along the top edge of the fabric, with the wrong side of the zipper facing up and matching the side edges of all the layers of fabric.

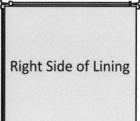

Lay the remaining lining piece on top, wrong side up and matching the top and side edges of the fabrics. Unzip the zipper a couple of inches so that the zipper pull will be out of the way of the presser foot when you sew. Pin all the layers in place. Sew ¼" (6mm) from the top edge.

Press all the fabrics away from the zipper along the seams (If you're using velvet, use your fingers to press the fabric instead of an iron). Topstitch the fabric along both sides of the zipper (see Basic Techniques: Sewing, Topstitch on page 147).

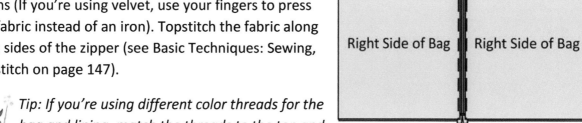

 Tip: If you're using different color threads for the bag and lining, match the threads to the top and bottom layers of fabric when you topstitch.

Sew the Side and Bottom Edges

Now we're going to sew the cover and lining fabrics together, but we're going to give special attention to the zipper so that it lies neatly in the finished bag.

Open the layers of fabric so that the bag pieces lie with their right sides together and the lining pieces lie with their right sides together. At one end of the zipper, pinch the two zipper tapes together so that the wrong sides of the zipper tapes face each other. Smooth the layers of lining fabric, and pin the layers of zipper tape and lining together. Do the same at the other end of the zipper.

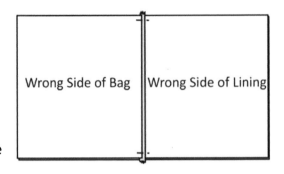

Baste across the ends of the zipper, 3/8" (1cm) from the edge, sewing through all layers.

Continue pinning the lining pieces together, right sides together, starting at each end of the zipper and moving toward the corners, matching the edges of the fabrics.

Pin the right sides of the bag pieces together, starting at each end of the zipper and moving toward the corners. Before you put in the final pins, reach between the layers of fabric and unzip the zipper about 6" (15cm).

Sew around the bag, 3/8" (1cm) from the edge, leaving a 4-5" (10-13cm) opening in the bottom of the lining.

Clip the corners and grade the seam allowances of the bag pieces.

Pull the bag right side out through the opening in the lining. Press (for velvet, finger press only).

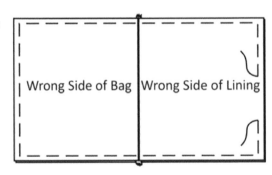

Close the Lining

At the opening in the lining, press the raw edges of the fabric in along the seam line. Stitch along the opening close to the folded edge, or sew the opening closed by hand with slip stitches (see Basic Techniques: Hand Sewing on page 147).

Push the lining to the inside of the bag.

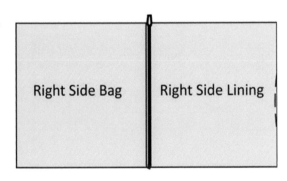

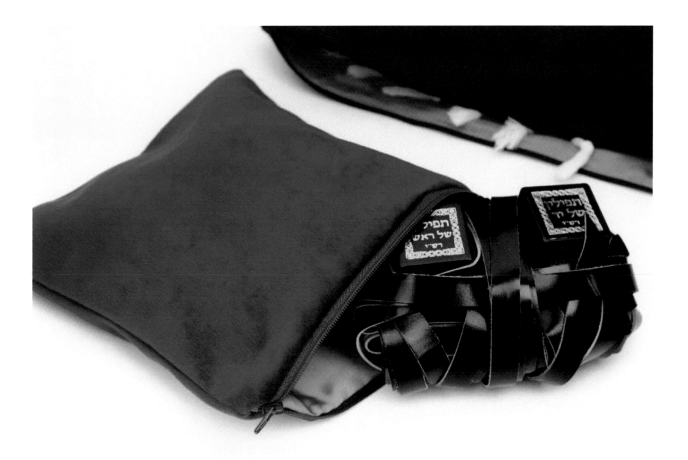

Tefillin Bag

Set Me for a seal on your heart, as a seal on your arm. (Song of Songs 8:6)

The tefillin bag might seem like just a mini version of the tallit bag, but it's perhaps much more special. Several classic Jewish texts say that the tefillin bag has the potential to become a holy object because it holds the tefillin. The tefillin are the leather boxes strapped to the arm and forehead during weekday morning prayers. They contain pieces of parchment printed with passages from the Torah. The pieces of parchment are sacred objects. Some authorities hold that the tefillin straps themselves are also sacred, which would make the bag that holds them holy, too. In fact, the Mishnah, a collection of commentaries on the Torah, says that the tefillin bag is one of only four objects that are important enough to be carried out of a burning synagogue on Shabbat; important enough that a person can break the Jewish laws that otherwise would prevent them from carrying objects outside on Shabbat (Shabbat 16:1). The other objects are a Torah scroll, a Torah wrap, and the tefillin themselves. This tefillin bag is a simple-to-make project with a very special purpose.

Finished size: 9¼" x 9¼" (23.5cm x 23.5cm)

Materials

*Recommended fabrics: **Bag:** Medium or heavy weight woven fabric such as velvet, canvas, twill, duck; **Lining:** Medium or heavy weight satin, cotton, or cotton blends*

Fabric:
> **Bag:** 3/8 yd. (30cm) at least 35" (90cm) wide
> **Lining:** 3/8 yd. (30cm) at least 35" (90cm) wide

9" (23cm) Zipper

Thread (As with the tallit bag, the threads will show in the finished bag. If your lining is a different color than the bag and you don't want contrasting threads to show against the fabric, use two different colored threads.)

Special Equipment

Pattern paper (For alternatives see Basic Techniques: Making Patterns on page 138.)

Hand sewing needle, size 6-8 (Optional, only needed if finishing the lining by hand.)

Instructions

Make the Pattern

Use the pattern paper to make a square pattern 10" x 10" (25cm x 25cm).

Cut the Fabric

Cut two copies of the pattern from the bag fabric and two copies from the lining.

Sew the Bag

Sew the bag using the instructions for the tallit bag (the previous project), beginning with attaching the zipper.

 Because a tefillin bag has a degree of holiness, when it becomes unusable it needs to be discarded in a respectful manner. Opinions differ on the degree of holiness of the bag, so check with your rabbi or other trusted source for Jewish law. Your advisor might say the bag needs to be buried or stored in a repository for sacred objects, called a genizah, or they might say to place it in a closed plastic bag before putting it with regular items to be discarded.

Home

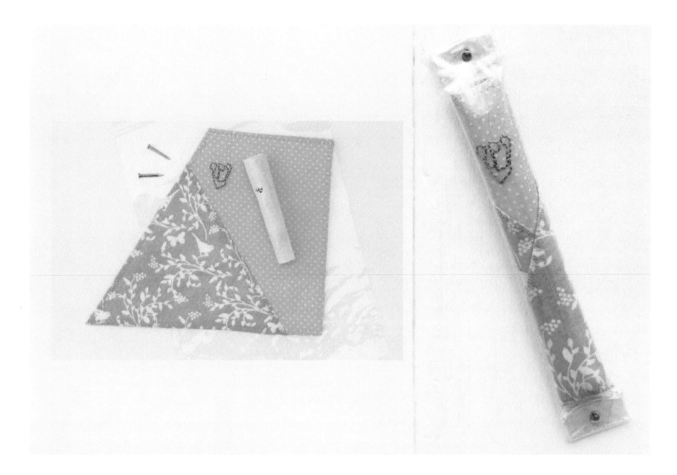

Mezuzah Case

This is the gateway of the Lord. (Psalms 118:20)

When you see a mezuzah on a doorpost of a house, you know the door belongs to a Jewish home. Within the outer case—often made of wood, metal, or stone—lies the mezuzah itself: a scroll of parchment on which Torah verses are written. We affix the verses to our doorposts to fulfill the Biblical commandment to "inscribe them on the doorposts of your house and on your gates" (Deuteronomy 6:9 and 11:20). The mezuzah scroll is a sacred object, and the mezuzah case that houses it is considered holy, too. I owe a big thanks to my friend Rivka for introducing me to a mezuzah case of clear wrapped vinyl. It's the perfect outer layer for this fabric-based mezuzah cover. The vinyl isn't sealed against the weather, so use the case on an inside doorway rather than on the outside of a home or building.

Finished size: Approximately 6" x 3/4" (15.2cm x 1.9cm)

Materials

Recommended fabric: Medium weight woven cotton and cotton blends, especially quilting fabrics; linen; Dupioni silk; jacquard

Fabric: For each component, use a fat quarter of quilting fabric **OR** the yardage/remnant size listed

Top: ¼ yd. (20cm) at least 35" (90cm) wide **OR** a 6" (15cm) square

Base (Darker in color than the top): ¼ yd. (20cm) at least 35" (90cm) wide **OR** a 7" (18cm) square

Fusible interfacing

Clear vinyl sheeting, 4mil thickness: ¼ yd. (20cm) **OR** an 8"x 5" (20cm x 13cm) remnant

Thread

Embroidery floss, cotton or polyester, in a color that contrasts with the fabric for the top

Purchased mezuzah scroll, 4" (10cm) long

Tip: Find vinyl sheeting at fabric shops or hardware stores.

Special Equipment

Water or air erasable fabric marker

Embroidery needle, size 5-10

4" (10cm) embroidery hoop

Flat head nails, in a size and type that works for the depth and construction materials of your doorway

Tip: The mezuzah shown in the photo is affixed to the background wooden frame with flat head linoleum nails. If you're not sure what size and type of nail would work best for your door frame, ask your local hardware dealer.

Instructions

Copy the Patterns

Copy or trace the patterns for the top, base, interfacing, and vinyl cover (for tips, see Basic Techniques: Copying and Tracing Patterns on page 137).

Cut the Fabric

Top Fabric: Cut one copy of the top pattern. Use the erasable fabric marker to trace the letter shin onto the right side of the fabric (see Basic Techniques: Transferring Pattern Markings, Tracing on page 139).

 Tip: The letter shin, the traditional decorative element on a mezuzah scroll case, stands for Shadai, one of the names of God. You'll notice the name spelled out on the back of your mezuzah scroll.

Base Fabric: Cut one copy of the base pattern.

Interfacing: Cut one copy of the interfacing pattern, placing the interfacing smooth side up and the pattern right side up.

Vinyl Sheeting: Cut one copy of the vinyl cover pattern.

Sew the Base and Top Together

With right sides together and aligning the notches, sew the base to the top along the notched edge using a ½" (1.2cm) seam allowance.

Trim the seam allowance to 1/8" (3mm). Press the seam allowance toward the base.

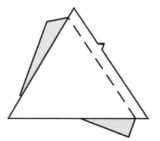

With the right side of the fabric facing up, sew along the seam line using wide zigzag stitches, so that the stitches lie mostly on the base but overlap the top slightly. Press along the seam.

 Tip: You can substitute another decorative machine stitch for the zigzag stitch.

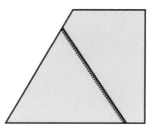

Embroider the Shin

Embroider the shin using the backstitch and two strands of embroidery floss (see Basic Techniques: Hand Embroidery, Backstitch on page 145).

Finish the Edges

Press under ½" (1.2cm) on all sides of the wrap.

Place the interfacing rough side down on the wrong side of the wrap, tucking it under the pressed edges. If necessary, trim the edges of the interfacing so that it fits inside the pressed edges. Use an iron to fuse the interfacing to the fabric, following the manufacturer's instructions.

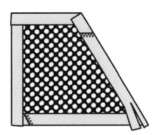

Trim the pressed edge to 1/8" (3cm).

Working with the right side of the fabric facing up, sew along the entire outer edge of the fabric wrap with wide zigzag stitches.

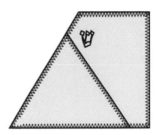

 Tip: Decrease the stitch width as you sew around the sharpest corner.

Wrap the Mezuzah Scroll in the Fabric Wrap

If your mezuzah scroll is not already rolled into a cylinder, consult a resource on Jewish practice for instructions on how to roll it up.

Lay the fabric wrap on your work surface with the wrong side up, the long edge closest to you, and the sharply angled corner to the right.

We're going to take a moment to ensure that when we roll the fabric around the parchment scroll the letters on the outside of the rolled scroll will align with the embroidered shin on the wrap. To do that, place the scroll on the wrap perpendicular to the long bottom edge and along the same line as the shin, as in the diagram. The scroll should lie equally distant from the top and bottom edges, with the letters on the outside of the scroll facing toward the fabric. Roll the scroll across the surface of the wrap to the left edge.

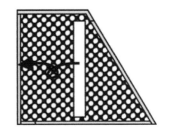

Now roll the wrap and scroll together to the right, making a tube, until you reach the end of the fabric.

Wrap the Mezuzah in the Vinyl Layer

Place the wrapped scroll along one long edge of the piece of vinyl, midway between the top and bottom edges. Roll the vinyl around it.

Make sure the long open edge of the vinyl lies at the back of the mezuzah scroll, on the opposite side of letter shin. If it doesn't, unroll the vinyl cover, adjust the position of the fabric-wrapped scroll, and roll it up again.

Affix the Mezuzah to Your Doorway

 Tip: Consult your rabbi or other trusted source for Jewish rituals for details about where on your doorway to affix the mezuzah as well as the blessing to recite.

Flatten 1" (2.5cm) of one end of the vinyl tube. Fold 3/8" (1cm) of the end of the tube to the back of the mezuzah case. Fold again to encase the raw end of the tube. Do the same on the other end.

When you are ready to affix the mezuzah to your doorway, recite the blessing and hammer one nail through the middle of each folded section of vinyl.

 Tip: Because a mezuzah case is a holy object, when it becomes unusable it needs to be disposed of in a respectful manner, either by burying it or placing it in a specialized storage called a genizah.

Pattern

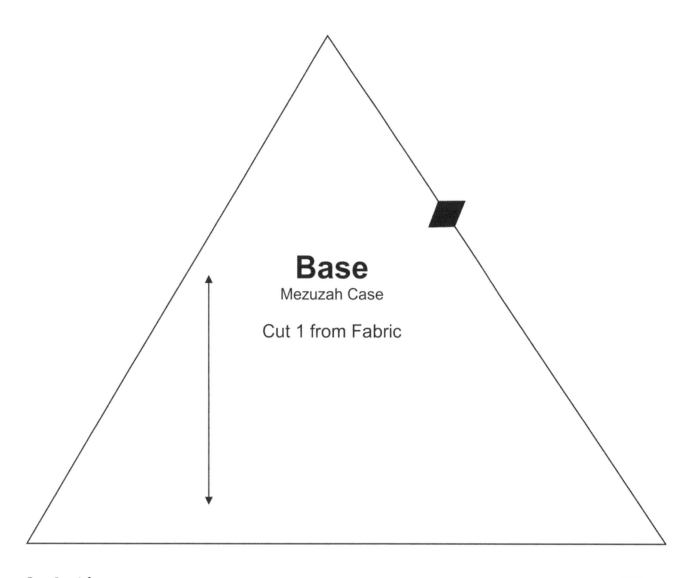

Base

Mezuzah Case

Cut 1 from Fabric

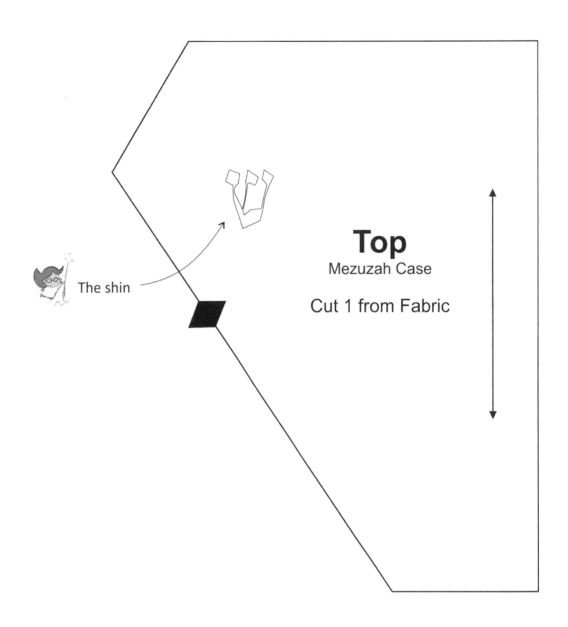

The shin

Top
Mezuzah Case

Cut 1 from Fabric

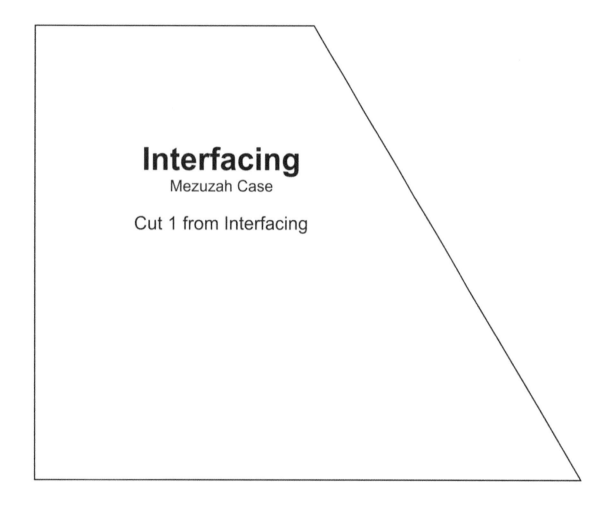

Interfacing
Mezuzah Case

Cut 1 from Interfacing

Vinyl Cover
Mezuzah Case

Cut 1 from Vinyl Sheeting

Tzedakah Jar Wrap

Hillel used to say, "The more tzedakah, the more peace."
(Pirkei Avot 2:8)

The Jewish word for charity, tzedakah, is closely linked to the concept of justice. According to the Talmud (Bava Batra 9a), giving tzedakah equals all of the other Biblical commandments combined. Past generations have passed on to us the custom of dropping a few coins into a tzedakah box—a *pushke*, in Yiddish—just before lighting candles for Shabbat or a festival. Here we have a variation on a tzedakah box: a tzedakah jar. The scene on the fabric wrap, with its lit candles and stars, suggests evening falling on a Shabbat or festival landscape. And as if giving tzedakah wasn't enough to make you feel good, you can make this project from reclaimed materials: a repurposed food jar and remnants from your fabric stash.

Finished size of fabric wrap: Varies with size of jar used

Materials

Recommended fabrics: Medium weight woven cotton and cotton blends, especially quilting fabrics; linen

Fabric: For each component a fat quarter of quilting fabric **OR** the yardage/remnant size listed

Background: See the first step of the instructions to determine the amount of fabric needed.

Hills applique: 1/8 yd. (10cm) at least 35" (90cm) wide **OR** 6½" x 2" (17cm x 5cm) rectangle

Candles, stars, and home appliques: 1/8 yd. (10cm) at least 35" (90cm) wide **OR** 3" x 4½" (8cm x 12cm) rectangle

Iron-on adhesive web

Thread

Jar with a smooth surface

Special Equipment

Spray adhesive that works with both glass and fabric

Instructions

Make the Background

Measure the circumference of the jar and add 1" (2.54cm). Determine how tall you'd like the wrap to be –keeping to the smooth, flat surface of the jar– and add 1" (2.54cm).

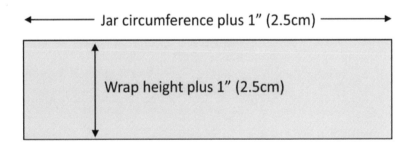

Cut a piece of the background fabric with these dimensions.

Make the Appliques

Use the fusible web to create appliques for the hill, candles, stars, and home. (or see Basic Techniques: Machine Applique, Making Appliques from Cotton and Linen Fabrics on page 140).

Arrange the appliques on the background fabric, keeping in mind that the outer ½" (1.2cm) on each edge will be turned to the back of the wrap. Remove the backing from the adhesive web, and iron the appliques to the background fabric using the instructions provided by the adhesive web's manufacturer.

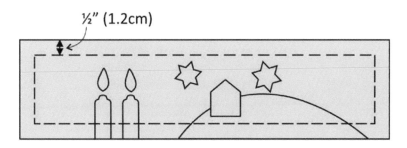

½" (1.2cm)

 Tip: You can always add more copies of the appliques, especially the stars, home, and hill, as you like.

Finish the Appliques

Finish the edges of the appliques with zigzag stitches (see Basic Techniques: Machine Applique, Finishing Machine Appliques on page 142). You don't need to finish the edges that line up with the edges of the background fabric.

 Tip: To create the folk art look of the wrap in the photograph, use a stitch length of 1 and a stitch width of 1.5.

Finish the Wrap Edges

Press under ½" (1.2cm) of fabric on all sides of the wrap. Trim the pressed edges to a width of between 1/8" and ¼" (3mm – 6mm).

Sew around all sides of the wrap with wide zigzag stitches.

Affix the Wrap to the Jar

Affix the fabric wrap to the jar with spray adhesive. When placing the wrap on the jar, start with the center of the wrap and move toward the edges, smoothing the wrap as you go and overlapping the ends.

Pattern

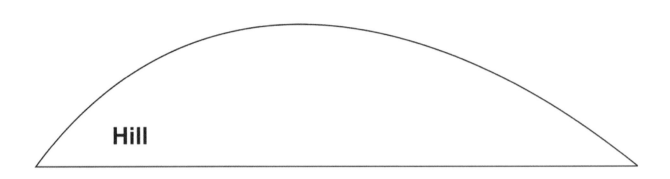

Hill

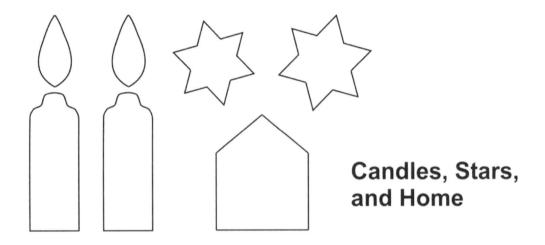

Candles, Stars, and Home

Mizrach

From east to west the name of the Lord is praised. (Psalms 113:3)

The Hebrew word *mizrach* means east. A mizrach is a traditional decoration that hangs on an eastern wall of a home to mark the direction of the Land of Israel, the direction to face when praying. Presumably, the tradition developed in communities west of Israel. Folk traditions consider the mizrach a symbol of God's protection. The charming scene in this version looks to the east across the rolling fields and meadows of an idyllic Promised Land.

Finished size: 5" x 7" (12.7cm x 17.8cm) not including the frame

Materials

Recommended fabrics: Medium weight woven cotton and cotton blends, especially quilting fabrics; linen

Fabric: For each component, a fat quarter of quilting fabric **OR** the yardage/remnant size listed

Background: ¼ yd. (20cm) at least 35" (90cm) wide **OR** 15" (38cm) square

Meadow applique: 1/8 yd. (10cm) at least 35" (90cm) wide **OR** 8" (21cm) square

Letter appliques: 1/8 yd. (10cm) at least 35" (90cm) wide **OR** 7" (18cm) square

Wheat field applique: 1/8 yd. (10cm) at least 35" (90cm) wide **OR** 4" (10cm) square

Orchard applique: 1/8 yd. (10cm) at least 35" (90cm) wide **OR** 4" (10cm) square

Stars and home appliques: 1/8 yd. at least 35" (90cm) wide **OR** 3" (8cm) square

Iron-on adhesive web

Thread

Frame at least 5" x 7" (Note that the mizrach in the photo uses a larger frame with a mat.)

Special Equipment

Water or air erasable fabric marker

 Tip: You don't need a different color thread for each applique. The version in the photos uses one natural-colored thread for the whole project, which makes the stitches stand out against the fabric and contributes to the informal, folk art appeal.

Instructions

Copy the Pattern

Copy or trace the pattern for the background at the end of the instructions (for tips, see Basic Techniques: Copying and Tracing Patterns on page 137).

Cut the Fabric

Background Fabric: Cut two copies of the background pattern from the background fabric. On one copy, use the erasable fabric marker to trace the all applique guidelines except the letters on to the right side of the fabric (for tips see Basic Techniques: Transferring Pattern Markings, Tracing on page 139).

Iron-on Adhesive Web: Cut one copy of the background pattern.

Make the Appliques

Make appliques for the orchard and wheat field using the applique patterns, fabrics, and adhesive web (see Basic Techniques: Machine Applique, Making Appliques from Cotton and Linen Fabrics on page 140).

Remove the backing from the adhesive web and position the appliques on the background. Iron the appliques onto the background using the web manufacturer's instructions.

Prepare the meadow applique, but before you remove the backing from the adhesive, use the fabric marker and the background pattern to trace the applique guidelines for the letters onto the right side of the meadow.

After tracing the guidelines, remove the backing and position the meadow applique on the background using the placement guideline and matching the bottom and side edges. Iron the meadow onto the background.

Prepare the letter, star, and house appliques, and iron them in place on the meadow and background fabrics.

Finish the Appliques

Finish the exposed edge of the orchard applique with zigzag stitches (see Basic Techniques: Machine Applique, Finishing Machine Appliques on page 142).

Finish the top edge of the wheat field.

Finish the top edge of the meadow, stopping and re-starting as necessary to avoid the letters and house.

Finish the edges of the letters, stars, and house.

Finish the Background Edges

Use an iron to press the mizrach from the wrong side of the fabric. Place the copy of the background pattern cut from adhesive web on the wrong side of the appliqued background fabric with the bumpy side down. Iron the applique to fuse it in place.

Remove the backing from the adhesive web, and place the second piece of background fabric on top of the web, with the wrong side of the fabric facing the web. Iron the fabric to fuse it in place.

Finish the raw edges of the background fabric with narrow or medium-width zigzag stitches.

Place the mizrach in the frame.

Pattern

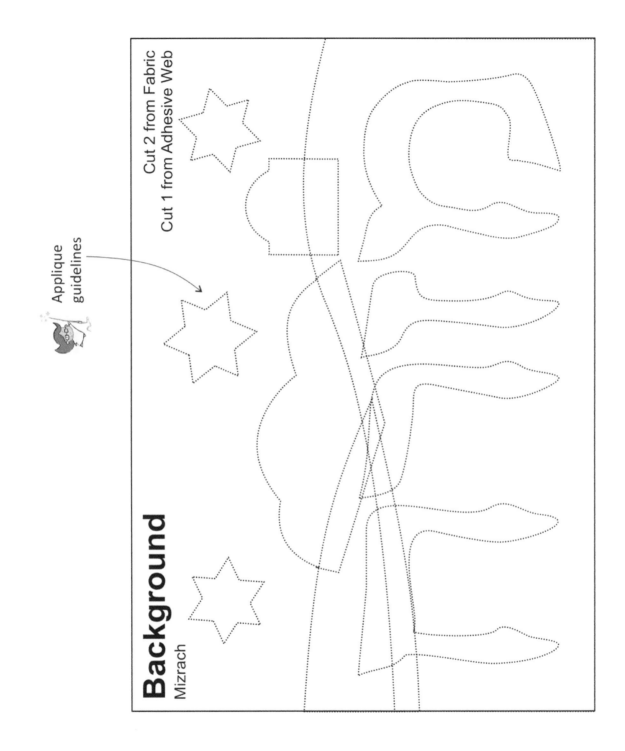

Applique guidelines

Background
Mizrach

Cut 2 from Fabric
Cut 1 from Adhesive Web

Appliques

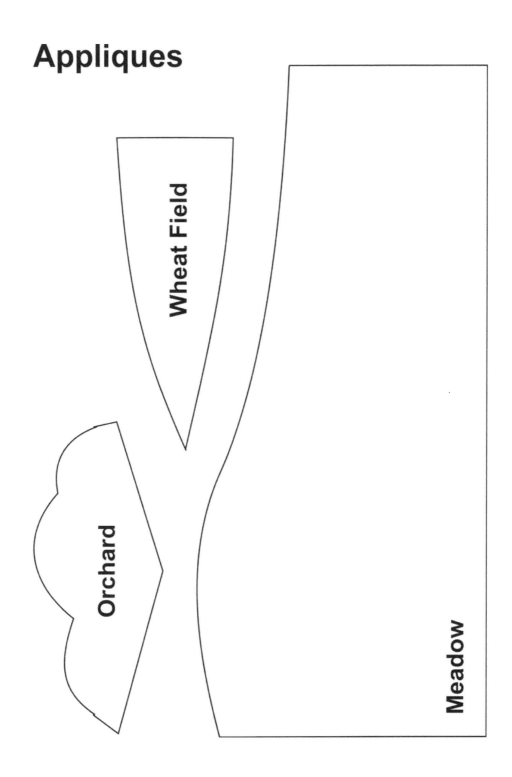

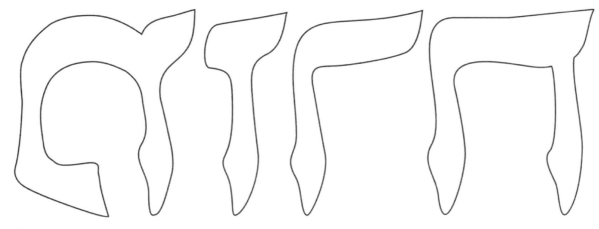

Letters

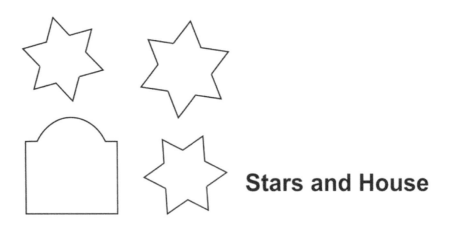

Stars and House

Sew Jewish

Hamsa

Your hand is strong. Your right hand, exalted. (Psalms 89:14)

A tiny falafel shop I used to frequent in London had a wall covered in hamsas in lots of different styles and materials. Every time I went in there I thought the shop needed one made from fabric. Like this one. The hamsa is an ancient symbol of good luck that comes to Jewish culture through the early Mizrahi and Sephardic communities of Mesopotamia and North Africa. It's also known as the Hand of Miriam, after Moses' sister, and represents God's protective hand or a hand swatting away the evil eye. Here, the hamsa is paired with fish, another symbol of good luck, and the Hebrew word *chai*, for "life."

Finished size: 5" x 5" (12.7cm x 12.7cm) not including the frame

Materials

 Tip: I created the hamsa in the photo with quilting materials for a folk art look, but you can also use silk or silk-like fabrics to create a look that's more formal. If you do, use fusible tricot interfacing instead of adhesive web, and follow the applique instructions in Basic Techniques: Making Appliques from Silk and Silk-like Fabrics on page 141.

Recommended fabrics: Medium weight woven cotton and cotton blends, especially quilting fabrics; linen

Fabric: For each component, use a fat quarter of quilting fabric **OR** the yardage/remnant size listed

 Background: ¼ yd. (20cm) at least 35" (90cm) wide **OR** 10" (26cm) square
 Hamsa applique: 1/8 yd. (10cm) at least 35" (90cm) wide **OR** 5" (12cm) square
 Fish applique: 1/8 yd. (10cm) at least 35" (90cm) wide **OR** 3" (7cm) square
 Letters applique: 1/8 yd. (10cm) at least 35" (90cm) wide **OR** 2" (5cm) square

Iron-on adhesive web
Thread
Embroidery floss
5" x 5" frame

Special Equipment

Water or air erasable fabric marker
Embroidery needle, size 5-7

 Tip: You won't need an embroidery hoop to hold the fabric when embroidering the fish details because the appliques will be stiff from two layers of adhesive web.

Instructions

Copy the Pattern

Copy or trace the pattern for the background (for tips, see Basic Techniques: Copying and Tracing Patterns on page 137).

Cut the Fabric

Background Fabric: Cut two copies of the background pattern. On one copy, use the erasable fabric marker to trace the hamsa placement line on the right side of the fabric.

Adhesive Web: Cut one copy of the background pattern.

Make the Appliques

Use the outline of the hamsa pattern to create an applique from the fabric and adhesive web (see Basic Techniques: Machine Applique, Making Appliques from Cotton and Linen Fabrics on page 140), but before removing the paper backing from the adhesive web, trace the letter placement guidelines from the pattern on to the right side of the applique.

After tracing the guidelines, remove the backing from the hamsa applique and position it on the background fabric. Iron it in place using the web manufacturer's instructions.

Use the outlines of the fish patterns to create appliques from the fish fabric and adhesive web. Before removing the backing from the adhesive web, trace the embroidery lines onto the right side of the appliques.

After tracing the embroidery guidelines, remove the backing from the fish and iron them in place on the hamsa.

Use the letters pattern to create appliques. Remove the backing from the adhesive web and position the appliques on the right side of the hamsa. Iron them in place.

Finish the Appliques

Finish the edges of the appliques with narrow zigzag stitches (see Basic Techniques: Machine Applique, Finishing Machine Appliques on page 142).

 Tip: Small appliques call for narrow finishing stitches. For the project in the photo I set the stitch width on my sewing machine to 1.5 and the length to 1.

Embroider the Fish

Embroider the fish details using doubled embroidery thread. Use the backstitch for the gills (see Basic Techniques: Hand Embroidery on page 144). For each eye, take two small stitches next to each other.

Finish the Background Edges

Press the hamsa from the wrong side of the fabric. Place the copy of the background pattern cut from adhesive web on the wrong side of the appliqued background fabric, bumpy side down. Iron it to fuse it in place.

Remove the backing from the adhesive web, and place the second piece of background fabric on top of the adhesive web, with the wrong side of the fabric facing the web. Iron the fabric to fuse it in place.

Finish the raw edges of the background fabric with narrow to medium-width zigzag stitches.

Place the hamsa in the frame.

Pattern

Background
Cut 2 from Fabric
Cut 1 from Adhesive Web

Applique placement line

Appliques

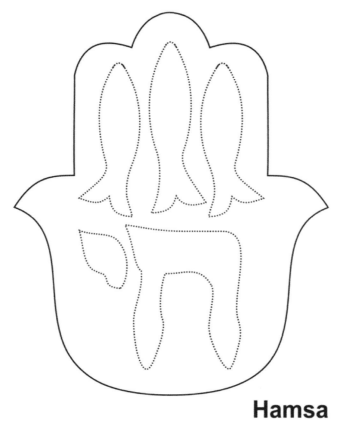

Hamsa

Embroidery lines
(don't forget the eyes!)

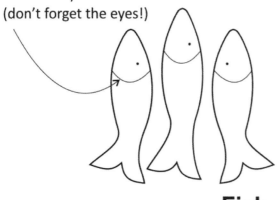

Fish

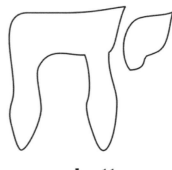

Letters

Shalom Pillow

May there be well-being within your walls, peace in your citadels. (Psalms 122:7)

Shalom! Peace! Bring a sign of peace into your home, and welcome guests with a hand-crafted version of the Hebrew greeting known across the Jewish world.

Finished Size: 9½" x 6¼" (23.5cm x 15.9cm)

Materials

Recommended fabric: Medium weight linen, woven cotton or cotton blend

Fabric: ¼ yd. (20cm) at least 35" (90cm) wide **OR** 1 fat quarter quilting fabric
Thread
Embroidery floss, cotton or polyester
Fill

Special Equipment

Pattern paper (For alternatives see Basic Techniques: Making Patterns on page 138.)
Water or air erasable fabric marker (If using light color fabric.) **OR** Transfer paper (For dark
    fabric.)
Embroidery needle, size 5-10
Small embroidery hoop
Hand sewing needle, size 6-8 (Optional, only needed if finishing the pillow by hand.)

Instructions

Make the Pillow Pattern

Use the pattern paper to make a rectangular pattern 7½" x 10½" (19cm x 27cm).

Cut the Fabric

Cut two copies of the pattern from the fabric.

Copy or trace the shalom embroidery pattern at the end of the instructions (for tips, see Basic Techniques: Copying and Tracing Patterns on page 137).

Transfer the shalom pattern to the right side of one fabric piece using the erasable fabric marker or transfer paper (see Basic Techniques: Transferring Pattern Markings on page 139).

Embroider

Embroider the design using a chain stitch and a double strand of floss (see Basic Techniques: Hand Embroidery on page 144). For each letter, bird or leaf, embroider the outline first, then embroider another line of stitches just inside the outline. Continue with more lines of stitches, each line inside the previous one, until the design is filled.

Sew Pillow Pieces Together

With right sides together, sew the pillow pieces together ½" (1.2cm) from the edges, leaving a 3" (8cm) opening on the bottom.

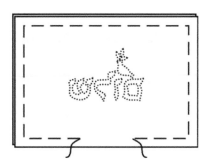

Turn the pillow right side out. Press the edges, turning in ½" (1.2cm) of fabric along the opening.

Stuff and Finish

Stuff the pillow with fill.

Stitch close to the edge of the pillow along the opening, or sew by hand with slip stitches (see Basic Techniques: Hand Sewing on page 147).

Pattern

Aleph-Bet Cuddle Blanket

By the breath of children God sustains the world. (Talmud Bavli, Shabbat 119b)

A collection of Jewish sewing projects has to include one project that highlights the Hebrew aleph-bet, and it has to have something for the little ones. This project is both: a cuddle blanket that introduces the next generation to the first three letters of the aleph-bet: aleph, bet, and gimmel.

Finished size: 30" x 40" (76cm x 102cm)

Materials

*Recommended fabrics: **Blanket:** Fleece (double-sided, washable and anti-pill, with a pile of not more than 3mm); **Appliques:** Fleece*

Fabric:

Blanket: 1¼ yd. (110cm) at least 35" (90cm) wide **OR** 7/8 yd. (80cm) at least 45" (115cm) wide

Appliques: 1/8 yd. at least 35" (90cm) wide **OR** 8" (20cm) square

1 pkg. (4¾ yd., 4.35m) polyester blanket binding

Thread

 Tip: You'll want to be able to wash the blanket from time to time, so make sure all your fabrics are washable.

Special Equipment

Pattern paper (For alternatives see Basic Techniques: Making Patterns on page 138.)

Instructions

Make the Pattern

Use the pattern paper to make a 30" x 40" (76cm x 102cm) rectangular pattern.

Cut the Fabric

Cut one copy of the pattern from the blanket fabric.

Attach the Binding

Notice that one folded side of the binding is slightly narrower than the other. Pin the binding to one edge of the blanket, starting near the middle. The narrow side of the binding should lie on the right side of the blanket, and the fold should lie right up against the blanket edge.

With the narrow side of the binding facing up on your sewing machine, use a zigzag or straight stitch to sew the binding to the blanket close to the binding's finished edge. Cut the threads, but don't cut the binding.

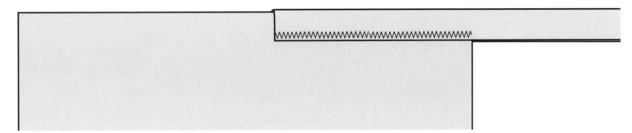

Pin the binding to the next side of the blanket, folding in the excess binding at the corner to make a neat 45 degree angle on both the top and bottom of the blanket.

Sew the binding to the blanket along the binding's finished edge as you did with the first side.

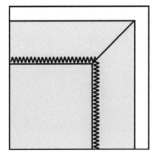

Continue sewing the binding around the edges of the blanket, but stop a few inches from where you began.

Cut the end of the binding 4" (2.5cm) beyond where the binding begins. Press 1" (2.5cm) of the binding to the inside. Press the two folded sides of the binding to the inside at a 45 degree angle. Pin the binding to the edge of the blanket.

Sew the remainder of the binder to the blanket, turning at the 45 degree angle and stopping at the blanket's outer edge.

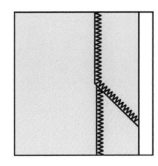

Add the Appliques

 Tip: Make sure all sewn items used by babies and children stay in good repair. If appliques and interfacings become detached or get chewed up by pets, repair them so they don't become choking hazards.

Copy or trace the aleph, bet, and gimmel applique patterns at the end of the instructions (for tips, see Basic Techniques: Copying and Tracing Patterns on page 137).

Cut one copy of each letter from the applique fabric.

Position the letters on the blanket and pin them into place.

Finish the edges of the appliques with zigzag stitches (see Basic Techniques: Machine Applique, Finishing Machine Appliques on page 142).

Pattern

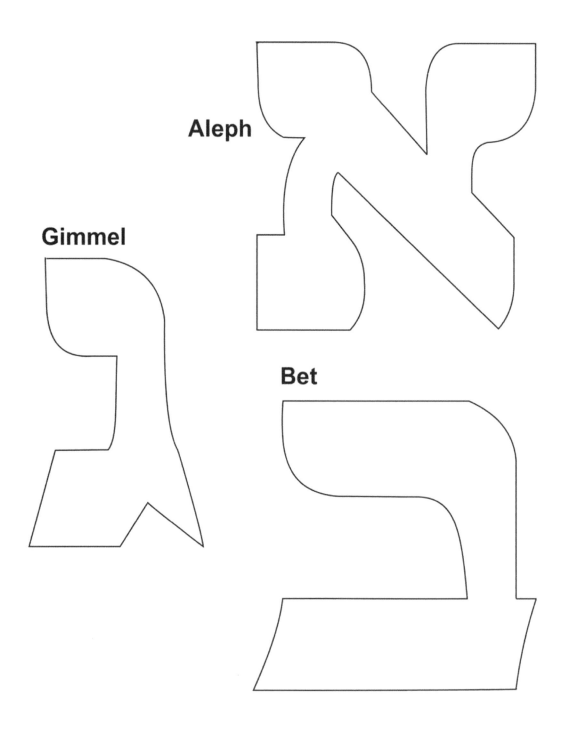

Aleph

Gimmel

Bet

Basic
Techniques

Choosing Fabric

With a world of fabrics available, how do you choose? The recommendations for each project will guide you to fabrics with characteristics to help make your project a success. For example, for the tallit bag I recommend fabrics that stand up to years of use. For the challah cover, we want fabrics that drape well. For the Purim mishloach manot boxes, we're looking for a material that lends structure.

Before buying fabric, make sure it is at least as wide as the minimum width given in the materials section. If choosing a wider fabric reduces the required yardage, the materials list includes yardages for more than one fabric width. Otherwise, just make sure the fabric meets the minimum.

Unless the instructions indicate, the yardages listed assume that the fabric has been pre-shrunk or that the finished product won't need to be washed. If you choose a fabric that shrinks more than average when washed, such as linen, and you expect to have to wash the finished project occasionally, you may need to buy additional fabric and pre-shrink it by washing and drying it before you cut out the pattern pieces. The salesperson at your fabric shop should be able to advise you.

Copying and Tracing Patterns

Reproduce the printed patterns by copying them with a copying machine or scanner or by tracing them onto tracing paper or freezer paper.

When tracing the pattern, be sure to trace the pattern markings such as dots, embroidery guidelines, and applique placement guidelines.

Some pattern pieces are larger than one page and are printed in pieces over several pages. After copying or tracing all the pattern pieces, cut them out and tape them together using the guidelines at the edges of the pieces. To help you put the pieces together, diagrams on the patterns show how the completed patterns should look.

Where the instructions refer to the right side of a sewing pattern, it refers to side of the paper on which the pattern is printed.

Making Patterns

When a pattern piece is a large square or rectangle, the instructions provide the dimensions to make your own. This way you avoid having to print out and tape together a lot of blank pages.

Most instructions call for making the pattern with pattern paper. Pattern paper, which comes as a large roll with a pre-printed grid for easy measuring, comes in especially useful for large patterns. You'll find it at fabric stores. For a less expensive alternative use a roll of gift wrap. It also often has a printed grid on the back.

For smaller patterns, you can use wax paper, parchment paper, or even pieces of scrap paper taped together. Avoid papers that have ink, like newsprint, or other substances that could rub off onto the fabric.

 Tip: Another option for making small square and rectangular fabric pieces is to use a rotary cutter and measuring grid—standard tools for cutting quilt pieces—to cut pieces of fabric in the required size and skip the pattern making altogether.

Cutting the Fabric

In the illustrations, the gray area represents the "right" side of the fabric, the side that will show on the outside of the finished project. For projects consisting of only one layer of fabric, such as the tallit, it's the side that faces up or faces out when the finished project is used.

White represents the "wrong" side of the fabric, the side that doesn't show in the finished project. For projects with only one layer of fabric, it's the side that faces down or in when the project is used.

Dotted areas represent interfacing or craft backing.

Avoid placing patterns on the selvage, the flat finished edges of the fabric.

If the pattern piece has a grain line—a long arrow—printed on it, position the pattern piece on the fabric so that the grain line lies parallel to the fabric's selvage, which is the fabric's finished edge.

Transferring Pattern Markings

Pattern markings serve lots of useful purposes. They help us line up pieces of fabric accurately. They show where to sew, hem, or fold fabric. Or they indicate where to embroider or place an applique. This book uses two techniques for transferring pattern markings to the cut fabric pieces: tracing and transfer paper. This section covers the types of pattern markings used in the book and the two transfer techniques as well as general tips that are useful for both techniques.

 Tip: Before using any transfer tool, test it on a scrap of fabric to make sure you can remove it using the instructions provided by the manufacturer.

Pattern Markings

| Small and Large Dots | Seam Allowance/ Hem Line | Fold Line | Applique Placement Guideline | Embroidery Guideline |

Transfer Techniques

Tracing

Tracing works well for transferring pattern markings onto fabrics that are lightweight and translucent. Lay the fabric on top of the pattern and trace the markings with an erasable fabric marking pen.

To help you see the pattern markings, you can put a piece of white paper on your work space under the pattern. You can also place the pattern and fabric on a light board or hold them up to a sunlit window.

A water or air erasable fabric marker fades naturally over time and disappears entirely when wet. If you notice that the markings are fading before you're done using them, use the marker to retrace them before they disappear entirely.

 If you don't have an erasable fabric marker on hand, you can often substitute a pencil, but take extra effort to draw the lines lightly to ensure the pencil lines won't show on the finished project.

Transfer Paper

Use transfer paper to transfer pattern markings if the fabric is heavy or if it's so dark in color that you can't see the pattern markings through the fabric. As with any transfer technique, try it out first on scrap fabric.

Choose a color that contrasts with the fabric so that you can see the markings easily; white paper for blue fabric, for example, or blue paper for yellow fabric.

Place the transfer paper between the fabric and pattern with the colored side down, facing the fabric. Use a tracing wheel and sufficient pressure to transfer the colored substrate to the fabric. In a pinch, you can use a ball point pen instead of a tracing wheel, but be sure you don't press down so hard that you rip the pattern and tracing paper and end up getting pen ink on the fabric.

General Tips

Dots are used to align two pieces of fabric. To transfer a dot easily and accurately, draw an "X" through the center.

When transferring long, straight lines, a ruler or other straight edge can help you keep the lines straight and accurate.

When transferring applique placement guidelines, you often don't have to transfer the entire outline of an object. Just be sure to transfer enough lines to make the position of the applique clear.

Machine Applique

Making Appliques from Cotton and Linen Fabrics

Notice that the applique pattern is the mirror image of the applique that appears on the final project. The design will get flipped during the process of making the applique and attaching it to the background fabric.

Start by tracing the applique pattern onto the paper side of iron-on adhesive web using a pencil or ball point pen.

Place the adhesive web onto the wrong side of the applique fabric with the shiny side facing the fabric. Use an iron and the manufacturer's instructions that come with the web to fuse the applique to the fabric.

 Tip: When fusing the applique to the background fabric, avoid sliding the iron across the applique or turning it in place. This can distort the applique or cause the edges of the applique to fray. Instead, pick up the iron to move it.

Cut out the applique.

Tip: If details are going to be added to the applique, such as embroidery or smaller appliques, this is usually the point where the instructions will have you add guidelines to the applique.

Peel the paper away from the back of the adhesive web. Position the applique on the background fabric with the adhesive side of the applique facing the background fabric.

Use the instructions that come with your adhesive web to fuse the applique to the background fabric.

Finish the raw edges of the applique according to the project instructions or as described in the section on Finishing Machine Appliques on page 142.

Making Appliques from Silk and Silk-like Fabrics

 Tip: The iron-on adhesive web that works for cotton and linen fabrics will make silk and silk-like fabrics stiff, so instead use fusible tricot interfacing. The interfacing seals the threads at the edge of the applique and helps keep them from fraying. However, unlike adhesive web, interfacing is only fusible on one side, so instead of ironing the applique onto the background fabric we need to baste it in place.

Notice that the pattern is the mirror image of the applique on the final project. The design will get flipped during the process of making the applique and attaching it to the background fabric.

Start by tracing the applique pattern onto the smooth side of fusible tricot interfacing with a pencil or pen using short, light strokes.

 Tip: Test the fusible interfacing on a scrap of fabric before applying it to your project pieces.

Place the interfacing on the wrong side of the applique fabric with the fusible side facing the fabric. Use an iron to fuse the interfacing to the fabric, using the instructions and heat guidelines that come with the interfacing.

 Tip: Before applying the iron to the applique, double check that the smooth side is up and the fusible side faces down. Otherwise, if the fusible side faces up when you apply heat, the applique could fuse to your iron.

Cut out the applique.

Pin the applique in place on the background fabric with the interfacing facing the fabric. Baste the applique to the background fabric with stitches that are about ¼" (6mm) from the edges, or—for narrow sections like the lines of Hebrew letters—down the middle of the applique.

 Tip: To give you more control when basting, use a stitch length of 3 or 4 rather than 5 to slow the machine.

Later, when the edges of the applique are finished, remove the basting stitches, working from the wrong side of the background fabric to avoid pulling threads in the applique.

Finish the raw edges of the applique according to the project instructions or as described in Finishing Machine Appliques, the next section. Use sharp needles in your machine—the package should specify "sharp"—to avoid leaving holes in the fabric.

Finishing Machine Appliques

Whether you make your applique with cotton, linen, or silk-like fabrics, finish the edges with zigzag stitches. The following sections cover choosing the stitch width and length, beginning and ending, and how to move around the appliques to give a smooth look to your stitches.

 Tip: If the project involves a number of appliques made from different colored fabrics, you don't have to buy thread to match all the fabrics. You'll notice that the projects in the book that have many appliques use either use the same neutral colored thread for all the appliques or two threads, one light and one dark.

Choosing Stitch Width and Length

Use the stitch width and length given in the project instructions, or choose the settings that produce the effect you want to create. The stitch width should be in the range of medium to wide. For the stitch length, choose a setting on the long side to create a folksy or informal effect, or shorten the stitch length to about 0.5 for a more formal look. The very close zigzag stitch created by this short stitch length is called satin stitch.

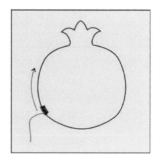

Test the stitch on scrap fabric before applying it to the project.

 Tip: If you're new to machine applique, try using a short stitch length to slow the machine and give you more control.

Beginning and Ending

Start by taking two to three straight backstitches.

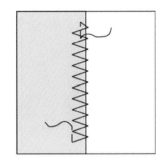

Set the sewing machine to the zigzag stitch, and select the stitch width and length. As you sew, the right side of the zigzag stitches should lie on the background fabric just to the right of the applique. Don't center the stitches on the edge of applique.

Finish with two to three straight stitches that lie just to the left of the zigzag stitches.

 Tip: When working on a particularly special project, create an extra neat finish by bringing the ends of the threads to the wrong side of the fabric, knot them, and trim the ends.

Turning Corners and Curves

As you sew along different types of corners and curves these techniques will help you create a smooth line of stitches without gaps.

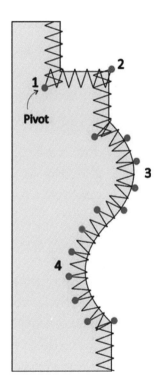

1. *Inside Corner (Turning to the Right):* Sew past the corner a distance that equals the width of the zigzag stitches, and stop with the needle in the fabric in the left position. Lift the presser foot, pivot the fabric, and lower the presser foot. Continue stitching.
2. *Outside Corner (Turning to the Left):* Stop at the corner with the needle in the right hand position. Pivot fabric. Continue stitching.
3. *Convex Curve:* Stop and pivot as necessary with the needle in the right hand position.
4. *Concave Curve:* Stop and pivot as necessary with the needle in the left position.

 Tip: Walk your machine one stitch at a time around difficult curves. Depending on the type of machine you use, turn the hand wheel or use the needle up/down button.

5. *Sharp Outside Corner:* As you near the corner, stop with the needle in the right hand position and switch to a narrower stitch width. Stop at the corner with the needle in the right hand position. Pivot. Take several additional narrow stitches. Stop with the needle in the right hand position and switch back to the original stitch width.

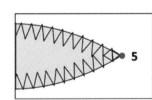

Tip: If you find yourself getting off track or you can see that the needle isn't going to fall where you want it to, you can raise the presser foot (after making sure that the needle is raised) and reposition the fabric slightly. Lower the presser foot again before you continue sewing.

Hand Embroidery

Equipment

For the projects in this book, I used cotton embroidery floss. You can also use polyester.

Choose a size 5-10 embroidery needle, also called a crewel needle. The eye of the needle should be large enough for the thread to pass through, and the shaft of the needle should be small enough that it doesn't leave visible holes in the fabric.

An embroidery hoop holds the fabric while you stitch. To hoop the fabric, start by separating the smaller and larger pieces of the hoop. Lay the fabric over the smaller hoop. Push the larger hoop down over the smaller one, catching the fabric in between. Make sure that the hooped fabric is taut and that the threads lie neatly horizontally and vertically. If the hoop is of the type that needs to be tightened manually by turning a screw on the side, do that now.

 Tip: Embroidery scissors, which have narrow blades and sharp points, are convenient for snipping the ends of the thread. They also come in handy when cutting the fabric from the center of tzitzit holes on a tallit.

Beginning and Ending

Cutting Single/Double Threads: Embroidery floss comes in skeins of six threads twisted together. Without untwisting the six threads, cut a piece that is 18"-20" (45-50cm) long. If you are going to embroider with a single strand, pull one thread from the six. Pulling down on the other threads and twisting them a bit between your fingertips helps. Thread the strand into the needle and pull it through at least a few inches or whatever length is comfortable for you as you stitch.

If you are going to embroider with double threads, remove two threads together. Thread them into the needle at the same time, or at least starting with the same end, so that the twists run in the same direction to create the best effect when you embroider. The diagrams in the book show one thread, so just treat the doubled thread as if it's a single thread as you work.

1. *Beginning:* Anchor the end of the thread by holding it close to the wrong side of the fabric and working it into the back side of the first few stitches.

2. *Moving Between Sections:* Avoid carrying the thread from one object to another across the fabric. Instead, begin embroidering each object with a new thread. However, you can move from one point of a design to another point that is only a short distance away without starting a new thread by bringing the needle to the wrong side of the fabric and weaving the needle and thread between the fabric and stitches.

3. *Ending:* To end a set of stitches, leave a few inches (10cm) of thread. Pass the needle and thread to the wrong side of the fabric and weave the remaining thread into the back side of the last stitches. Trim the thread.

Backstitch

This stitch creates a solid line.

Bring the needle up through the fabric near the right side of the line to be embroidered, at A (see the illustration), one stitch length away from the end of the line. Put the needle down through the fabric at the right end of the line, B, and bring it up one stitch length away from A, at C.

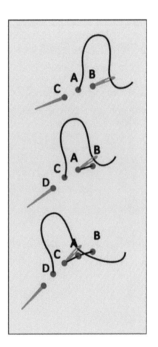

To make the next stitch, put the needle down through the fabric at A, and bring it up one stitch length away from C, at D. For the best effect, try to keep the stitches the same length.

Continue in the same way, starting each new stitch by inserting the needle into the fabric at the point where it last emerged from the fabric.

 Tip: For the projects in this book, use a stitch length of about 1/8" (3cm) or slightly longer.

Chain Stitch

Use this stitch to make a line or fill an area.

Bring the needle up through the fabric on the right side of the line to be embroidered, A.

Hold the thread down with your left thumb, above and the to the left of A. Insert the needle close to A and bring it up a stitch length away, at B.

Pull the needle through to create one loop in the chain. The needle should pass over the top of the trailing end of the thread, as in the diagram, so that the stitch will form the shape of a loop. As you finish the stitch, don't pull the thread so tight that you lose the chain link shape.

To make the next stitch, insert the needle inside the first link, near B, and bring it up again another stitch length away, at C. Continue, starting each new stitch inside the previous loop. Keep the stitch length even as much as possible.

Anchor the last loop with a short straight stitch.

Sewing

General Information

Use a seam allowance of ½" (1.2cm) unless the instructions indicate otherwise.

On most sewing illustrations in this book, the only stitches shown are the stitches for the current step.

Baste

Basting stitches are long, straight stitches used to hold two pieces of fabric together temporarily or to mark the position of a line. Set your machine to a stitch length of 4 or 5. Longer stitches will be easier to remove, but with shorter stitches your machine will move more slowly and you'll have more control.

Basting stitches can be removed after they've served their purpose or left in place if they're not visible in the finished project.

Topstitch

Stitch on the right side of the fabric, usually close to a seam or fold.

Clip the Corner

Use scissors to trim some of the seam allowance where a seam turns a corner. Be careful not to cut the thread of the seam.

Clipping the corner reduces the bulk of the seam allowance so that it lies flat in the finished project.

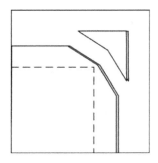

Grade the Seam Allowance

Use scissors to trim the layers of fabric of a seam allowance. Trim the fabric layers of the seam allowance to different widths, but avoid trimming any layer to a width of less than 1/8" (3mm).

Grading removes bulk from the seam allowance, allowing it to lie flat in the finished project or allowing your machine to sew over the seam allowance more easily in a later step of the project.

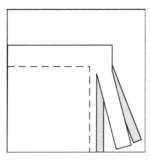

Hand Sewing

For the hand sewing in this book, use a needle size of 6 to 8 for the best results. Use the thread type specified in the instructions or the same thread you used for machine sewing.

Cut a piece of thread about two feet (50cm) long. Thread it through the eye of the needle, bring the ends of the thread together, and knot the ends together about ½" (1.2cm) from the ends.

Running Stitch

Pass the needle up and down at equal intervals through the layers of fabric or trim. A typical stitch length is about 1/8" (3mm), but you can adjust the length based on the materials you're working with. If the fabric allows, you can make more than one stitch at a time, passing the needle up and down through the fabric a number of times before pulling it through the fabric with the thread, as in the diagram.

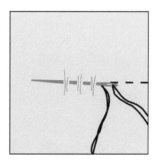

Slip Stitch

Use the slip stitch to close the openings in seams from the right side of the fabric. Start with the seam allowances pressed to the inside of the project along the seam lines.

Bring the needle up through the seam line of the lower layer of fabric on the right side of the area to be stitched.

Insert the needle into the seam line of the upper layer of fabric just above the point where the needle emerged from the lower fabric, and bring the needle out again ⅛"- ¼" (3mm-6mm) away.

Take another stitch in the lower layer of fabric, starting just below the point where the needle emerged from the upper layer, as in the illustration. Try to keep the stitch length uniform. Continue until the entire opening is sewn closed.

When the seam is finished, knot the thread close to the fabric. To hide the ends of the thread, pass the needle through the seam and bring it up through one of the layers of fabric. Pull the thread so that the fabric puckers slightly, and trim the thread close to the fabric, being careful not to cut the fabric. The end of the thread will slip back underneath the fabric for a neat finish to your project.

Tallit Information Sources

For more details about the Jewish laws and traditions behind the tallit, look for these books at your favorite bookseller or Judaica shop.

A Guide to Jewish Prayer, Rabbi Adin Steinsaltz
Schocken Books, New York

Tzitzith: A Thread of Light, Rabbi Aryeh Kaplan
NCSY/Orthodox Union

Kitzur Shulchan Aruch—The Code of Jewish Law (Vol. 1—Simanim 1-34), Rabbi Shlomo Ganzfried
Mesorah Publications, New York

About the Author

Maria Bywater is the designer behind Huppahs.com, the leading national wedding huppah rental company.

She converted to Judaism in her mid-twenties. While living in North Africa, the Persian-Arab Gulf, and London, she became inspired to explore Jewish cultures and traditions through needle crafts.

Maria now lives in New York's Mid-Hudson Valley with her two daughters amid a large extended family.

She writes about Judaism and sewing on her blog, Sew Jewish. Visit SewJewish.com.

Acknowledgements

Creating this book has been a long journey, and I'm grateful to so many people. I want to especially thank:

Agnes and Clara, for filling my life with joy.
My whole extended family, especially Steve and Mandy and their family, for all their support.
Joe and Alanna for their support and generous use of their home for photos.
Ann Redelfs, for her guidance and support.
Rabbi Michael Shire and Rabbi Marcia Plumb, who encouraged me to start.
Judy, Michael, Cathy, and Glenn, who helped me find my home in Judaism.

www.sewjewish.com

DISCARD

CPSIA information can be obtained at www.ICGtesting.com
Printed in the USA
LVIW01n1322090217
523752LV00004B/28